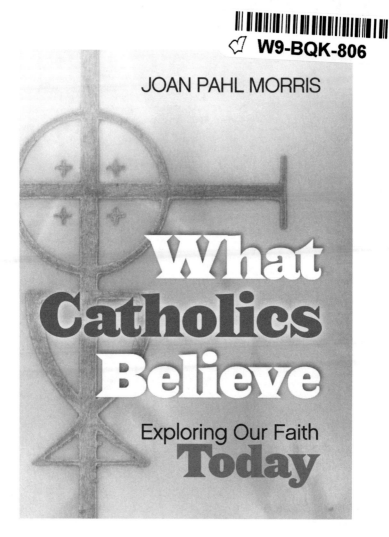

JOAN PAHL MORRIS

What Catholics Believe

Exploring Our Faith Today

TWENTY-THIRD PUBLICATIONS

185 WILLOW STREET • PO BOX 180 • MYSTIC, CT 06355
TEL: 1-800-321-0411 • FAX: 1-800-572-0788
E-MAIL: ttpubs@aol.com • www.twentythirdpublications.com

Second printing 2005

Twenty-Third Publications
A Division of Bayard
185 Willow Street
P.O. Box 180
Mystic, CT 06355
(860) 536-2611 or (800) 321-0411
www.twentythirdpublications.com
ISBN:1-58595-263-X

Library of Congress Catalog Card Number: 2003104398
Printed in the U.S.A.

Contents

INTRODUCTION

This book is an outgrowth of years spent in the challenging dialogue of religious education. I have worked as a parish director of adult religious education, been a participant or leader in numerous Bible study and prayer groups over the years, and taught religion in Catholic high schools. Certain questions and topics have come up repeatedly, either because they are central to Christian teachings, or because they pose a particular problem in the minds of many believers. I have frequently heard the complaint that church teachings are confusing, artificial, or don't make sense. And trying to be cooperative, people will often say, "It's just a mystery, and we're supposed to take it on faith."

Let me address that last statement first. Good News is meant to be understood! It's not good news to me unless I understand it. But we are often working with dated or technical language from church documents of earlier centuries, not to mention biblical writings which are thousands of years old and translated from foreign languages and equally foreign cultures. Also, writings of previous centuries reflect a pre-scientific worldview. Today we need to be able to state our Christian faith in ways compatible with the scientific assumptions of the modern believer. The good news has not changed, but language is constantly changing, and the experiences that provide cultural reference points are always changing. As Christian believers, we need to find ways of putting our traditional beliefs into language that makes sense to us as adults in our world today.

Restating beliefs in new language should not be seen as a threat. We do not really understand any concept until we can put it in our own words. And it is especially important for teachers, catechists, and preachers to be able to put those traditional teachings into modern everyday language, so that we can effectively announce the Good News to others.

This is not a comprehensive introduction to Christianity for new believers. The focus is a few key concepts frequently questioned by the teens and adults with whom I have worked and prayed over the years. The book is particularly for those raised as Catholics, who already have considerable familiarity with traditional Catholic teaching, but are now searching for an adult understanding of the teachings they memorized years ago. Many Catholic adults find themselves recalling grade-school answers when religious questions arise, and of course, to an adult those answers now sound childish and unsatisfying. I suspect that this is frequently the reason religion is thought to be childish. Most Catholics ended their religious education before they were grown, and think that grade school answers are all there is to Catholicism.

This book will also be especially useful for lay catechists and teachers who are encountering and trying to answer the questions of their youngsters. It would be ideal for small faith groups who want to discuss something of substance but don't want to tackle textbooks. It could also be used as a supplement with senior high students or catechumenate programs when the group is asking certain questions, though it is not suitable as a basic text. For something more comprehensive, there are many fine books available: introductions to Catholic teachings, or general reading on particular topics such as the Bible or sacraments. I do give a few suggested readings at the ends of some chapters. I have also indicated possible discussion questions for study or small faith groups at the end of every chapter.

My own background is Catholic, I am responding to questions from a primarily Catholic audience, and my training is Catholic, including an MRE (Masters in Religious Education) from The Catholic University of America. That Catholic focus will be very evident on some topics. However, much of what is written here reflects fairly common Christian beliefs and questions, so much of the time I refer to "Christians" or "the church," meaning the Christian tradition in general, not exclusively the Catholic church.

I also frequently refer to the "Hebrew" or "Jewish" Scriptures, rather than the "Old Testament." This is to emphasize our roots in the Jewish faith, and to respect that faith for itself. Occasionally you will see other authors refer to the "First Testament," meaning the same books. This change of words is to avoid any suggestion that the revelation to the Jews is now obsolete. Maybe "old" was an unfortunate word for us Christians to use! At the same time, let me note that the Christian Old Testament is not identical to the Jewish Scriptures. (There is further explanation of this in chapter 3.)

Readers will find few references or citations other than Scripture verses for two reasons. The first is that I did not do research to write this book. It is a selection of topics which I have taught innumerable times, so the ideas are as natural to me as breathing. The primary immediate reference I used is the *New American Bible with Revised New Testament*, Confraternity of Christian Doctrine, Benziger Publishing Co. 1986. Occasionally I also refer to the Baltimore Catechism, which was very widely used in the United States for decades, through the 1960's. Most Catholics over 45 or 50 years of age will remember it, since we memorized the questions and answers over and over through grade school. There was more than one version over the years. I was looking at *The Illustrated Revised Edition of the Baltimore Catechism No. 2 with Study Lessons*, Copyright 1945, 1962, by W.H. Sadlier, Inc. In the 1920's, my father had essentially the same questions in an earlier version, without additional study lessons.

The other reason I don't give a lot of references is that the interpretations of Scripture and theological ideas expressed here are widely held, and will be found in Bible footnotes or other appropriate sources. I have, of course, studied the work of many theologians over the years, but could not begin to credit any particular sources for my ideas, since these ideas have taken shape over more than twenty-five years' time. My goal as a teacher has been to restate commonly accepted theology so that it makes sense to those who never studied theology. Sometimes I create new images to express the message, but I do not intend to create any new theological interpretations.

Finally, of course, I must thank those who assisted me. Special thanks goes to the theologian Dr. Monika Hellwig, who is a fellow parishioner at my parish church. I was already well aware of her work, having used a couple of her books with my high school students in the 1980's. Dr. Hellwig read the first draft of this book, and gave me some constructive suggestions which, hopefully, I have followed! Special thanks also goes to my friend Dennis O'Malley, who went through a draft with a proverbial "fine toothed comb" and made many helpful comments. I also thank Fr. Vince O'Brien, S.J., Mary Jean Pavelko, and other friends who offered useful insights.

CHAPTER ONE

Faith

Contents

This chapter will look at what we mean by the word "faith," and what we believe about faith. The second section considers that very important concern about questioning one's faith. The last subtopic is a short explanation of the concept of "religious mystery," followed by a poem I wrote for my high school students years ago.

One subject that sooner or later comes up in every religion class or Bible study is the question of faith. Many of us have siblings or children who are not practicing their childhood faith. We wonder: Why do some people have faith, and others not? Why does one child in the family accept faith as his or her own, while another, seemingly brought up with the same experiences, rejects it and refuses to go to church? Is questioning my beliefs unfaithful? And do unbelievers go to hell?

We say that faith is a gift from God. If faith is a gift, why doesn't God give it to all? Or does God offer it, and it goes unrecognized or rejected? And if God is a good God who loves all people, why doesn't God make it possible for everyone to believe? We pray for the gift of faith, because faith makes life better. Even doctors are now beginning to report that people with a firm religious faith heal better.

What Is "Faith"?

Our first challenge is to clarify what we mean by "faith." In the Roman

Catholic tradition, people have tended to equate faith with the acceptance of the truths or beliefs taught by the Catholic church. Often this is called "the Faith." (The Nicean Creed, used as part of Sunday Mass and the sacraments of initiation, would be the best example of a statement of such core beliefs. The Creed was written in the fourth and fifth centuries.) But many people think of faith more as an attitude of trust. This may be particularly important in our rapidly changing modern times, when it is not uncommon for people to have a basic attitude of faith, or trust, in God but also have many doubts about traditional beliefs. (I would suggest that often the problem is that they have not heard the traditional teaching in words that make sense to them. It may be the language that they are rejecting, not the belief.)

If faith is first an attitude of trust, where does it come from? Modern psychology has given us a new understanding of the complexity of human experience. Though several children grow up in the same family, with the same parents, the same schools, and pretty much the same environment and major experiences (as far as an outsider can tell) their perceptions are different. Each child in the family has a unique position within the family, and personal relationships with each other are always different. Each person has their own set of friends and personal experiences. And it is a well-known phenomenon that after observing the same event, individuals recall various memories of what really happened. Even our genes probably predispose us to certain outlooks, causing one person to be more trusting and another more fearful, or making one more inclined to be open-minded and another prone to be conservative. In short, there is no way to answer the question about why some people have faith and others don't. We just recognize that each person's experience of life is unique, and though we may seek to nurture faith, it is ultimately a gift. A person can choose to listen, but this is not a guarantee of belief. Parents can do their best to nurture faith, but they cannot guarantee that their children will believe.

While we might decide to define faith as fundamentally an attitude of trust, it does also involve particular beliefs about God, God's will, and what is good and right. We have to respect each individual's beliefs. That does not mean we agree that each person is equally correct, or that something is true for one person and not for another. Believing that the earth is flat does not make it flat. And to say that the earth is flat for some people and round for others is obviously absurd. There are objective realities. If God exists, then

God exists, whether people believe in God or not. If lying or killing or marital unfaithfulness are evil, then they are evil, destructive, whether a person agrees or not. But we can still respect each individual's efforts to find the truth himself because when we get into matters of faith, we go beyond what can be proven. Proof is part of the scientific world, the world of material things that can be weighed and measured. Even within a church or community of believers, people differ in their beliefs. (Is God more like a man? A woman? Both? Neither? Is killing always wrong? If not always, when?)

Sincere people often ask why they should take anyone else's word on matters of religion. If we cannot prove that God exists, how is anyone to know what is true? The first answer is that the word faith implies a lack of proof. If we could prove these things, there would be no need for trust. If we could prove these things, then every person of good will would accept them as proven facts. Faith is believing what cannot be seen. But blind faith is no virtue. It would be foolish to believe everything we are told. We need some kind of evidence to know what to believe.

Many people find evidence of God easily available. For example, the beauty of nature or examples of human goodness have prompted popular quotes frequently seen on cards, banners, and such: "All that I have seen teaches me to believe in what I have not seen," or "The hand of the Creator is seen in creation." These ordinary experiences can be evidence, signs of God's presence. Every time we trust a friend, we are showing faith, based on the trustworthiness which that person has shown before. Marriage is an act of faith that the beloved will continue to be a loyal and loving partner. And again, we expect a person to wait for good evidence of trustworthiness before having enough faith to marry someone!

At times people have been led to believe that Jesus is the Christ, the anointed one of God, because of the witness of other Christians. Sometimes it has been the personal witness of one or two individuals. Usually it includes the example of a supportive church community and the written testimony of the Bible. In some way, each new believer has been touched and convinced by the witness of fellow travelers who seem to have found the way. Christianity is a community of faith.

In considering the mystery of faith, I sometimes ask people to imagine that someone hands them an old, unmarked box full of jigsaw puzzle pieces. This represents the challenge to have faith. You have no proof that the pieces all belong to one puzzle, or that the pieces are all there. But if a friend you trust tells you that it's a really neat puzzle, you might have enough faith in your friend to spend the time trying to put the puzzle together. Faith is that leap beyond what is known for sure.

People of good will do not always believe. In the Bible there are stories of people who were clearly good, believing Jews and who never recognized Jesus as the Messiah, the Christ. Paul's teacher, the rabbi Gamaliel, is an example (Acts 5:33; 22:3). Gamaliel served God according to his Jewish faith, and the Bible clearly portrays him as a good person, though there is no indication that he ever became a follower of Jesus.

Most Christians today believe that any person of good will who serves God as best they know how, is saved. We believe that our Christian faith is a gift enabling us to see God especially well, and trust that God is reaching every person of good will in other ways.

For centuries, many Christians did not believe this. Taking the necessity of baptism too literally, Christians often doubted that unbaptized persons could get to heaven. (I remember grade school classmates in the 1960's who were worried about this. I also clearly remember the teacher assuring us that God would save sincere non-believers.) Theologians knew this fear was contrary to our belief in a loving God, and had tried to resolve this seeming conflict in our teachings by defining concepts such as "baptism of blood" and "baptism of desire." "Baptism of blood" referred to a martyr's death. This teaching said that if a person had never been sacramentally baptized "with water and the Spirit" but had died for the faith, God would accept the person as a baptized person. (Thus, the person could go to heaven.) "Baptism of desire" referred to people who had not been sacramentally baptized but sincerely wanted to be good people and do God's will. It seems simpler just to say that we trust that God saves all people of good will. We recognize baptism and the other sacraments as powerful ways to experience God's presence in our lives, but we also realize that God is not limited to acting within our church celebrations. We are blessed to have the sacraments as a means to celebrate and encounter God's saving presence, but God reaches beyond our celebrations. God is God! The church does not have God trapped in a holy water bottle! We have faith that God reaches out to all people, and it is not for us to try to judge who is saved.

Is It Okay to Question My Faith?

Sometimes people who have a strong faith fear that questions are a sign of weakness. Questions are actually a sign of growth. Who has not heard the young child confidently proclaim, "It's true, Mommy said!" or "Teacher said!" Little children accept things without question, for a short while. But children soon learn that not everything they are told is actually true. Children, who in the past accepted everything, must eventually question it all in order to make it their own. This is especially evident during the teen years, but some people don't give religion much thought during those years, and have to come back to the task of re-examining their religious beliefs later, maybe decades later. Some people who are very religious also avoid questioning their faith because they are afraid of doubts or consider doubts disloyal. Decades ago, many Catholics thought they were not supposed to question the church. They thought they were supposed to take things on faith, which meant to accept teachings without questioning. This "Father knows best" attitude was perhaps in part a reflection of the immigrant church in the United States. When Catholic immigrant communities first settled here, the priest was commonly one of the few well-educated individuals in the community, and that situation exaggerated the deference shown to priests. Many people got into the habit of just taking a priest's word for everything, and of not feeling any need to try to understand church teachings themselves.

Today we realize that questioning is healthy. Questioning means a person is thinking. I have to question the beliefs I have been given to figure out if they make sense to me. If I have not thought about my faith enough to put it into my own words, then I do not really have a grasp of it; it is not really my belief yet. If I never question my faith, it will never truly belong to me, and I will not be able to apply it to my life on a practical day-to-day basis.

If a person is serious about his or her beliefs, questioning is not optional; sooner or later a person must question. A person who wants to hear the word of God must have an attitude of openness to new ideas. Not the openness of a garbage can that accepts everything, but a critical mind that carefully weighs what is offered so as to choose what is good and discard what is nonsense. God gave us brains; God expects us to use them.

Now, anyone who does grocery shopping knows that no matter how carefully you select the fruit, you occasionally get home and realize you have a rotten piece. Sometimes we will discover that something we used to believe no longer seems to make sense, and we must discard that belief. Christians must continue a lifelong search, praying, studying, and learning from each other, to better understand God's will. And from time to time, we must acknowledge with humility that, as individuals or as a believing community, we have been misguided, and our beliefs have been in error. Faith is an unfinished business. We begin with a basic attitude of faith in God's goodness and faith in the Spirit working through the church. Then this attitude of faithfulness must guide us in figuring out how to live day-to-day as Christians in our world.

Religious Mystery

We sometimes refer to certain religious teachings as "mysteries." This is another one of those words that has different meanings and can cause confusion. In popular use, mystery indicates something that is unknown. But when we speak of religious mysteries, we mean something quite different. We mean something that is known but not fully understood because it is too profound to grasp all at once. We refer to something not entirely explainable; we try to explain, but ultimately it is beyond our words. So no matter how much studying a person has done, each person ultimately must discover these mysteries for him/herself. Religious mysteries call for prayerful attention. If we say God's love is a mystery, or the union of God and man in Jesus is a mystery, we do not mean these are totally incomprehensible. We mean they are amazing realities of immeasurable depth. They are much more than simple facts that can be memorized and "known." We are challenged to ponder these awe-inspiring, wonder-full spiritual realities ever more deeply, that we might grow in understanding as we contemplate them day after day and year after year. Religious mysteries are meant to be understood. What value is there in claiming to believe something we do not understand? That seems pointless. What does it even mean? While we may never fully grasp the implications of God's self-gift to us, we can grow in our appreciation of God's life-giving, loving kindness. And as we grow in understanding the wonderful reality of God's presence, our faith will transform us more and more to God's life-giving ways, which lead to our fulfillment and happiness.

Years ago, I posted this poem on my classroom wall:

> To My Students...
> On Faith
>
> You're given a box full of peculiar-shaped pieces
> And told to assemble them one by one.
> You're told there's a picture, a beautiful treasure,
> Well worth the time and effort it takes.
>
> "But," you ask, "how can one know what is hidden
> In this chaos of strange and exasperating pieces?
> How can one know there is a picture? And what picture?
> What coherent whole awaits the seeker?"
>
> No one's puzzle is entire, it's true,
> But some, in juggling the pieces, see patterns;
> From clues sense the whole, and thus blessed,
> Work with confidence in the picture, as yet unseen.

Discussion Questions:
• What is my faith story? Where do I see myself in my faith journey? How did I come to faith, and when?
• Have there been times I wasn't sure what I believed?
• How do I encounter God? What symbols speak to me of God's presence?

Suggested Reading:
Catechism of the Catholic Church. English translation for the United States of America, United States Catholic Conference, Inc./Libreria Editrice Vaticana, (Boston: St. Paul Books & Media, 1994). This is the official catechism of the Catholic Church, with a detailed list of teachings in four areas; the creed, sacraments, moral life, and prayer. Useful for verifying official teaching of the Catholic Church. However, it is rather formal in its approach and would probably not be considered spiritually enriching by most readers.

CHAPTER TWO

The Church

Contents

This chapter is a short overview of the church community's sense of what it means to be church, noting differences in our sense of identity through history. Some of the most common views of the mission of the church, the job the church is supposed to be doing, are briefly noted in the following pages as well. (This largely reflects a widely circulated book by the theologian Avery Dulles, S.J., called *Models of the Church*. Father Dulles identifies five models or ways in which the church is viewed, and looks in depth at how these different assumptions affect all aspects of church life.)

Some religions, such as Buddhism, focus solely on the individual and his or her communion with the divine. Christianity, in contrast, sees other people, the church community, as a central element in our relationship with God. We come to know Christ through the church community, and by becoming part of that community we inherit the community's mission of being Christ to others.

The church is many things. It is not only a faith community. It is also an institution in the world, sometimes with civil power as well as religious authority. The mission of the church has been seen differently at different times and places in history. Within the church we have had considerable conflict over what the church should be and what the individual believer's role is within the church. This chapter will briefly touch on some major differences that have been seen through history. The church is constantly growing and changing in its sense of self-identity, even as it strives always to be faithful to its roots in the teaching of Jesus.

In the first few centuries, the early church was a small community of believers in a larger and often unfriendly pagan world. The culture was unchristian, but people could generally worship the gods of their choice, as long as they also accepted the civil religion, emperor worship, which was considered essential to hold the empire together. Under some emperors, the Christians were persecuted because they would not offer the required worship to the emperor. Surrounded by this larger pagan culture, the early Christians saw themselves as a family, a community, nurturing and supporting each other and sharing in a mission to "be Christ to others" by bringing the Good News to the world. There was not yet a well-developed institutional structure. Authority tended to be recognized by the local community, based on competence. Rules were few, and they varied from community to community. We see this kind of church in the New Testament writings, written in the first and perhaps early second centuries.

Once Christianity became the state religion under the Roman Empire, profound changes took place. The church became both the uneasy partner and the rival of the emperors and kings, a situation that lasted for centuries. The church acquired all the trappings of power, status, and authority, which were vested in individuals with official roles, particularly the bishops. More and more the church was seen as an institution ruling under God and, for a long time, in partnership with kings and state authorities, who also were considered to rule under God's authority. This authority system, ruled by king and pope, was often proclaimed to be identical with God's authority and will. The institutional church was believed to speak for God, whereas in the early church the community as a whole prayerfully discerned the will of God. This difference in understanding is one of the things that eventually led to the split between the Roman church, modeled after imperial authority, and the Eastern churches, which continued to put greater emphasis on community and collegial discernment.

Becoming a state religion meant that within a short time nearly all the members of society were at least nominally Christian. As a result, being Christian ceased to be distinctive, and the sense of being a special community with a special mission diminished. "The church" began to mean the institution and its clergy, not the community of believers. Centuries later, many of the Protestant groups that broke away were trying on some level to reclaim that sense of community as church. (This was not the concern of all breakaway groups. Henry VIII's Church of England was a rival institution with the same kind of hierarchy that the Roman church had, just a different head authority, the king instead of the pope.)

The Catholic Church has been trying to reclaim the dignity and participation of the whole community since the reforms of the Second Vatican Council in 1962–1965. However, profound change always comes slowly. We Catholics currently experience considerable conflict over these two very different models for church and the implications they have for power and authority within the church.

This community/institution also struggles to identify its mission or job. The community model, which currently seems to be a strong ideal in many U.S. parishes, tends to emphasize fellowship, support, and taking care of its own members. (This may in part be filling a need the larger society does not fill. Families are scattered, and many people don't have any other community.) The institutional model tends to emphasize the job of governing, in which making and enforcing rules becomes central. Our western or Roman Rite, structurally modeled after the Roman government, has always had a strong emphasis on governing and laws.

In contrast to these two models, some people see the church's mission as primarily mystical and sacramental, bringing humankind into communion with God through worship. The Eastern Rite churches tend to emphasize this aspect of our faith. Some people emphasize the prophetic mission to preach and teach, bringing God's truth so that people might have the knowledge to accept God's ways as their guiding light. Many Protestant churches focus on this prophetic element of the Christian mission, and engage a lot of energy in preaching and witnessing. Then there is the servant role, which includes the traditional practices of feeding, healing, and giving practical physical assistance to people in need. More recently, this servant role has included the task of "building the kingdom," the social justice mission of restructuring laws and social policies to create a society that offers justice and peace to all. Social justice programs promote many "self-help" projects to empower the disadvantaged; "teaching a man to fish instead of just giving him a fish," as the saying goes.

All of these missions can be found in the Bible. They are all part of what it means to be church. We are constantly challenged to find the proper balance in living as Christians, both as individuals and as church communities. This is especially true in our modern age of rapid social change, which is causing change in the church itself. How should we use our time and resources? Should the church spend most of its money and energy taking care of its own members? Providing faith formation? Reaching out to others? How vocal should the church be in preaching God's word in a secular society? Do we confine our preaching to the church building, for the believers who want to hear it? Or do we stand on street corners, lobby Congress, or otherwise address the larger public? At what point do we have a Christian duty to protest unjust laws? Should our protest be confined to words, or should we be arrested for "disturbing the peace" of business-as-usual at sex businesses, abortion clinics, executions, nuclear weapons sites, or other legal activities our church finds morally offensive? A hundred and fifty years ago, Quakers broke the law by harboring runaway slaves. Now we honor the courage of the people who staffed this "Underground Railroad." Their action is what is called "civil disobedience," deliberately breaking what they believed to be a gravely sinful law. They risked arrest, of course. What is our view of civil disobedience? And how do we address justice issues within the church?

Being church is not easy, and Jesus did not give us specific rules. We begin with a clear biblical directive to choose life; to heal and reconcile and announce the kingdom as Jesus did. However, we have to figure out the details through prayer, study, and work with our fellow believers, knowing that we will not always come up with perfect answers, but that we must strive to be faithful and allow the Spirit of God to work through us.

Supposedly a reporter once asked Mother Teresa whether she became discouraged because of the number of people she was not able to help, and her answer was that God did not call her to be successful, God called her to be faithful.

We are only learning to be faithful. We are a flawed church. One symptom of that is the fact that the Christian church is fractured into many denominations. We are a church in progress. We are striving to "be Christ to the world," but we are not fully redeemed ourselves; we are still striving to become Christ's body. That calls for humility and a posture of listening, even as we proclaim God's Good News with confidence in the guidance of the Spirit.

Discussion Questions:

• How do I see my mission as a Christian?

• What understanding of church seems to guide activities at my parish? Do we need to grow in our understanding of our mission as the body of Christ community?

• Can we gain any insights about our modern church from a study of the Acts of the Apostles? (This book in the New Testament is about the early church.)

• How should we be Christ to the world in a secular society? Should we preach publicly? Protest? Try to change laws? Openly practice "civil disobedience," breaking laws we consider seriously contrary to God's law? (Public civil disobedience risks jail, of course.)

• How is our situation like that of the early Christians, who were very conscious that they were a small community in a larger non-Christian culture?

• How are we unlike the early Christians?

Suggested Reading:

Raymond E. Brown, SS., *Biblical Reflections on Crises Facing the Church* (Mahwah, NJ: Paulist Press, 1975). Still timely, solid but very readable reflections on the church and changes in teachings since Vatican II, by this well-respected Catholic scripture scholar.

Avery Dulles, S.J., *Models of the Church* (Garden City, New York: Doubleday & Company, Inc., 1974). This book has been very widely circulated, and the author's five "models," or ways of seeing the church, have become common reference points for many other speakers and writers.

For those especially interested in the issues of feminism or women in liturgy:

Marjorie Procter-Smith, *In Her Own Rite: Constructing Feminist Liturgical Tradition* (Nashville: Abingdon Press, 1990). The author is a teacher of liturgy at Southern Methodist University, Dallas, Texas. She brings feminist issues into dialogue with the study and practice of liturgy, and sees feminism as a natural partner assisting the ongoing liturgical reform of the Christian churches. She asks basic questions about things as fundamental as our language about people and God, and how that language shapes what we believe.

Understanding the Bible
A Basic Premise

Contents

Because there is much to cover, the subject of how to understand the Bible will be dealt with in three chapters, in an effort to keep each chapter a manageable length for discussion. This first chapter, Chapter Three, will establish a basic approach to reading the Bible and address the question of what we mean by saying it is the word of God. Chapter Four further explores literary forms, writing styles, and the authors' intent. Chapter Five looks at prophets and predictions.

Chapter Three addresses the challenge of understanding God's word in Scripture, and the way we address that challenge today. It begins with a quick review of different translations, then looks closely at the statement that the Bible is "the Word of God in the words of men." The last section briefly reflects on what we know of the authors of the Bible and the process through which the Bible took shape.

Clarifying the Problem

The Bible is of unquestioned importance to the Christian community, but it is also the subject of considerable conflict. The Bible is the word of God. It reveals God's truth to us. This is the basic premise or assumption of all believers. But Christians debate what the Bible reveals about God or our future. And in a scientific culture, believers are often uncomfortable with the seeming conflict between biblical faith and scientific knowledge. There are fundamentally different ways of reading the Bible, based largely on our concept of the Bible as literature. That is where we need to begin. What do we mean by "the Bible," and what do we believe about how God communicates to us through its human writers?

Which Bible?

It is easy to be confused by the variety of different Bible translations available. All the major Christian churches would agree that no additions or changes are to be made to the "original" Bible, which took shape in the first few centuries after the death of Jesus. So what are we to make of the different Bibles we find?

To review basic facts, we should note that the Christian Bible has two major parts: the New Testament, which includes the Christian books written in the century after the death of Jesus, and the Old Testament, essentially the Jewish Scriptures.

The Christian Old Testament is not identical to the Jewish sacred Scriptures, however. Christians rearranged the Jewish books to better express the Christian view that God's old covenant with the Jewish people had prepared for and predicted the new covenant established by Jesus. But this has led to some unfortunate misunderstandings of Christian belief. Many Christians have considered the Old Testament to be obsolete or even misguided or untrue. This is contrary to authentic Christian tradition. Almost three-quarters of our Christian Bible is Old Testament. We haven't been copying and printing all that paper for two thousand years for nothing! We Christians still believe that the Jewish books of the Old Testament are part of God's revealed word to humankind.

The number of books included in the Bible depends on the version. Catholics and Protestants use the same 27 books in the New Testament, but the Old Testament list differs. To oversimplify somewhat, this is essentially what happened. The early Christians generally used the Septuagint, a collection of the Jewish Scriptures written in Greek. At that time, Greek was the international language of the Mediterranean world. After the rise of Christianity, the Jewish community stopped using the Septuagint and went back to using only the books originally written in Hebrew. This meant they rejected seven later books in the Septuagint that had been originally written or preserved in Greek in the last centuries before Jesus. Then, as part of the Reformation, the Protestant churches went back to the Hebrew list of books for their Old Testament also. The Catholic Church has continued to use the full list from the Septuagint, which had been approved as part of the Bible in the early Christian councils long before the Protestant Reformation. Consequently, Catholic Bibles today have seven more books than other Bibles. Those seven books are often referred to as the apocryphal (meaning "hidden") or deuterocanonical (meaning "second canon" or second official list) books. (Another note of confusion: In the popular use of the word, any writing or story not accepted as true may also be called "apocryphal," so in popular use "apocryphal" means "not true.")

Even when we are speaking of the same books, translations will vary. Under the best of conditions, translation from one language to another is not an exact science. (This topic is further developed in the next section.) Through the centuries, Christians have translated and re-translated the Bible from the original languages into Greek, then Latin, and then from Latin into European languages, and from these languages into more modern versions, as each language, such as English, changed through time. Two well-known Bibles that are the result of this process of repeated re-translation through the centuries are the Catholic Douay-Rheims Bible and the Protestant King James Bible.

However, in the last century or so, archaeologists have found some very early biblical texts. Also, modern studies in history, archaeology, and languages have given us a far better understanding of biblical times than anyone has had since then. These discoveries have enabled recent scholars to do entirely new translations from the earliest known texts of the Bible, bypassing other translations done through the centuries. Also, biblical scholarship today is often a joint activity, with cooperation between Catholic, Protestant, and Jewish scholars. As a result of all this scholarship, these new versions are more accurate translations than the Douay-Rheims or King James.

The translation generally used in Catholic liturgy in the United States today is *The New American Bible* (NAB), so this version will sound very familiar. This is one of the completely new translations, published in 1970. Translators produced an even more recent version in 1986, The *New American Bible with Revised New Testament*, to eliminate sexist language. (Sexist language is often only a peculiarity of English, or of our language habits, not necessarily a part of the original writing.) This version has not replaced the first NAB as the official translation for liturgical use, however.

There are also other modern translations, such as the *New Revised Standard Version* (NRSV), which have the respect and approval of Catholic and mainline Protestant churches. The NRSV is actually the one used most often by scholars, Catholic or Protestant. The *New Jerusalem Bible* is another version considered acceptable, though not as widely used in the U.S. (This is not by any means an exhaustive list. These are some of the best known translations. There are others, and additional new translations are in process.)

Serious students of the Bible should avoid two kinds of translations. First, outdated versions such as the Douay-Rheims, which may include the old family Bible, lack the considerable advantages of twentieth-century scholarship. Second, some recent Bibles such as *The Good News for Modern Man*, *Today's English Version*, or *The Living Bible*, which were designed to be easy reading, may be fine for personal prayer but are not suitable for study. These are very free translations, more properly called transliteration. They might be compared to *Readers' Digest* condensed books. You cannot properly study any writing based on a simplified or condensed version!

For some further insights into the process of biblical translation, I would particularly recommend reading the two prefaces at the beginning of the New Testament in *The New American Bible with Revised New Testament*.

Where We Stand Today

We often hear the question "Is everything in the Bible true?" Christians all agree that the Bible is God's word and is therefore true, but we can mean very different things by that common affirmation. Part of the confusion lies in the fact that there are profoundly different ways of understanding how to read the Bible. Fundamentalist Christians believe that every statement in the Bible is literally true. The Catholic Church and many Protestant denominations now believe that much of the Bible was never meant to be taken literally. Such a conclusion is based on many kinds of evidence. Some of the evidence is found in the Bible itself, as well as in other areas of study.

That makes the job of understanding the Bible a little more difficult. We have to ask, "What does it mean?" not simply, "What does it say?" Biblical scholars have learned to use all the tools of modern scholarship to assist in their search for God's messages in Scripture. They study the ancient languages, of course, but they also use the methods of modern literary and historical studies. They analyze literary forms and the style of each author, and look for clues from history and archaeology to help them understand what the authors were talking about. And if we begin with the assumption that all truth must agree, and we believe that science is also a search for the truth, then we must also be able to reconcile our beliefs about the Bible with our scientific beliefs. (Yes, I use the word "belief" for both religion and science. Scientists may believe something to be fact, and later discover they were in error, just as we may discover that some of our beliefs about the Bible are in error. A genuine search for truth requires a humble willingness to reexamine our beliefs.)

Most people today are well aware that evidence from science and history appears to clash with biblical stories. For example, there is no way a scientific person can take the story of Noah's ark as literal fact. The world contains entirely too many species of animals to put on any boat. (We are still discovering new species!) It would be impossible to adequately feed and care for them. Besides, any species that is reduced to only a few individuals loses its genetic viability and is likely to die out, and the evidence doesn't show any possibility that such a worldwide genetic loss ever occurred. All plants also would have to be rescued. Even if some were seeds, can you imagine the cataloging challenge? And how were Noah and family to collect this incredible menagerie, and then return them to their proper continents and islands? Not to mention the lack of any evidence of a worldwide flood in the geologic record, and so on. In short, there is abundant physical evidence that there was no such flood. This is not debatable. There have been catastrophic floods in many local areas. Maybe even a super-catastrophic flood creating or enlarging the Black Sea. Such floods may have seemed like world-destroying floods to the people who lived there, and those memories could have been the beginning of ancient flood stories.

But if we don't accept the story of Noah's ark as literal history, what are believers to make of the biblical story? What message from or about God are we supposed to find?

There are two categories of evidence that help us judge how to understand biblical writing. One kind is external evidence, such as science, history, other literature, or any other source outside of the Bible. Believers will also want to look at internal evidence, evidence in Scripture itself, to see what the authors intended. For example, in studying the story of Noah's ark, we note that there are two versions of the story. In one version, Noah was to gather two of every animal, but in the next chapter a second version says seven pairs of every clean animal, and one pair of every unclean animal (Gn 6:19–20; 7:2–3). Our popular traditions have conveniently ignored the conflicting verses.

Many stories in the Bible are told more than once, with details in one version that undeniably contradict another version. In the Jewish tradition, it seems that there were two separate sets of the early stories told in Genesis. Modern scholars have concluded that the Jewish religious leaders wove together one set of stories from the Northern Kingdom and one set from the Southern Kingdom. (Actually they identify four separate sources that were eventually combined into the Hebrew Scriptures. See "The Pentateuch" in the introductory materials at the beginning of the *New American Bible*.) Those respected Jewish religious leaders who got together to decide what went into their sacred Scriptures put those contradictory verses together, without any attempt to mesh them or explain the contradictions. Obviously, they did not consider the differences a problem. If the contradictions were not a problem, then the religious leaders must not have taken the stories literally. This is just one of those internal clues that help us understand how to read the Bible. Modern literature studies have enabled us to identify many different types of literature in the Bible, and to realize that much of it was never meant to be literal history. There are historical facts in the Bible, but there is also much that is not.

Understanding the Bible is not easy. Translating ideas faithfully from one language to another is always a challenge, and biblical translation is greatly complicated by the age of the original material. Languages are constantly changing. Idiomatic expressions or secondary meanings can come and go very quickly. (Consider the change in meanings of "cool," "gay," "neat," or "bad" over a few decades.) Previously recognized symbols or expressions may disappear from common use and no longer be recognized. Cultural assumptions and common experiences change. (How many young adults today know what an "icebox" is? Or understand the world in which their grandparents grew up?) Biblical writers were not trying to be mysterious. A statement may have been perfectly clear when written, but be incomprehensible or badly misunderstood centuries later. Biblical translation encounters many such challenges, and we don't even have the original writings. Not that many Christians could read the originals if they were available. The Christian writings were primarily ancient Greek, read only by a few scholars today. The oldest existing copies of Scripture are centuries newer than the originals would be, and may themselves be translations. Because of all this, we find ourselves with odd situations like the three different endings for the Gospel according to Mark. (See the footnotes for Mark chapter 16 in *The New American Bible with Revised New Testament*.) Mark may have originally ended with verse 8, or his original ending may be gone. (The verse numbering was added centuries later.) Two other endings are included as part of our Bible today, and another is mentioned in the footnotes. Why do we have three or four endings? Several different early versions of Mark's gospel were found. We don't know which, if any, is the original version. So we don't know how Mark's gospel originally ended, or when the later parts were added. However, we do know that our present version, with multiple endings, has been approved by the church as God's inspired word.

And finally, since most of us cannot read the original languages anyway, we depend on further translation into our own language. It can be very instructive to compare a couple of the more accurate translations of the Bible, such as the *New American Bible* and the *New Revised Standard Version* of the Bible, and note the differences in the translations of the same passages.

All of this uncertainty may sound scary. Does it mean that everyone is guessing at the meaning of God's word? No, we are not left to figure it out ourselves. Faithful translation and explanation of the Bible is an ongoing work, and will continue to be needed as long as languages continue to change. (Though we should not assume we fully understand it. Records from two thousand years ago are meager. There will undoubtedly always be questions about accurate translation.) But as believers, we have confidence, faith, that the same Holy Spirit who guided the preaching of the apostles and the writing of the evangelists continues to guide the church in preserving and interpreting the message of God in our sacred Scriptures. For the layperson, there are many good commentaries and study books available, and any Bible designed for study has copious footnotes on troublesome passages, as well as introductory essays giving helpful background for understanding each book.

"The Word of God in the Words of Men"

One of the traditional ways we have summarized our faith in the Bible is by saying it is "the Word of God in the words of men." But what does this mean? Try rewriting that statement, removing "Word" and "words" and substituting other language. I sometimes use this exercise with classes or groups. After everyone has written a new statement, we compare results so as to come up with statements that seem generally acceptable. For "Word of God" people have used "meaning," "message," "truth," or "guidance." For "words of men" we have substituted terms such as "stories," "languages," "literary forms," or "cultural attitudes."

The goal of the exercise is to clarify that we do believe the Bible contains God's word, which is true. But we also realize that the message is presented in a variety of forms, which often should not be taken literally. The message is also contained in the work of human authors, whose writing skills and knowledge of history and science were sometimes limited. The authors speak from the cultural presuppositions of their own times; for example, that God approved of commonly accepted customs such as the slaughter of enemy babies, or of slavery, or of the subjugation of women. (Which cultural presuppositions of our time blind us to God's truth?)

THE BIBLE IS THE WORD OF GOD...	...IN THE WORDS OF MEN
meaning	stories
message	languages
truth	literary forms
guidance	cultural attitudes

In recent years, some authors have analyzed God and written and spoken about how God changed his mind, was conflicted, or matured in his behavior toward humans. This is completely inconsistent with the Christian understanding of God. The biblical stories about God differ, but that is because the human understanding of God changed. Our belief is that God is eternal, unchanging, perfect, and all good.

As we read the Bible, to avoid being misled by the limitations of a human author, we have to evaluate a particular statement in light of the whole Bible. The word of God is always a message of life and liberation. That would be our first clue. If a statement does not seem to be life-giving, does not sound like good news for all, then we have not discovered God's word in it. Our God is the God of life. Sinful people that we are, we modern readers, like the ancient writers, have a tendency to assume that God approves of our own culture, customs, or cause in war. But the liberating word of God keeps popping up in the words of prophets and holy people, challenging the kings, the powerful, the status quo. We believers need to keep listening! There is a lot of wisdom in the Bible that Jews and Christians both have been slow to fully recognize.

A good example for Christians is the statement by Paul, "There is neither Jew nor Greek, there is neither slave nor free person, there is neither male nor female; for you are all one in Christ Jesus" (Gal 3:28). That first-generation church to whom Paul spoke, which had begun as a community of Jewish followers of Jesus, was sharply divided over whether gentiles (often called "Greeks" in the Bible) could be true Christians, full members of the church communities. Many of the first Christians, who were devout Jews, believed that God wanted a Christian convert to first become a Jew and follow the Jewish way of life. They saw Judaism as the basis for Christianity. After all, Jesus was the Jewish Messiah, was he not? Jesus himself was a practicing Jew. Those Jewish Christians had always considered their religious laws, such as circumcision and kosher eating, to be God's will. The Christian church settled that question, at least in theory, within the first generation. But some of the early Jewish Christians broke away when gentiles were accepted as equal members. (See Acts 13:43–45.)

What of the other divisions that Paul mentions? It was nearly two thousand years before Christians stopped justifying slavery. In the U.S., up until the past generation, many churches continued to blatantly justify racist attitudes. Equality between the sexes is still an unresolved issue. Some Protestant denominations accept women ministers, while many sincere Christians remain convinced that God intends women to be under male dominion. (In Genesis 3:16, this male domination is seen as part of the disorder caused by sin, not part of God's original plan.)

Scholars continue to work to better understand biblical authors, their world, their languages, their literary styles, and the symbols and expressions they used. It is very important to understand what the human authors were trying to say, because God's messages are contained in the human authors' messages. The only valid meaning in any writing is the meaning intended by the author; in this case, the various human authors and editors, as well as the divine author. We are not free to interpret the Bible any way we want. We can never add new meanings to someone else's work. We may discover meanings we did not previously recognize, but that is not through some private revelation out of the blue. (An individual may experience prayerful and valid private insights prompted by their reading, but we cannot say that those private insights are part of the meaning of the written word.) Discovering the meaning in the Bible is done through careful scholarly study of the clues that point to the intentions of the original authors, and to the intentions of the church leaders when they carefully selected and put together these works and declared them to be sacred Scripture.

Individual Authors and the Authoring Community

What do we know about the authors of the Bible? A good study Bible will explain what is presently known about the author and writing style in an introduction at the beginning of each book. Scholars, studying the writings in their original languages, find many clues that identify an author and the author's background. Identifiable individuals wrote some of the biblical books. For example, scholars are confident that Paul is the actual author of many of the epistles. We are also confident that the prophet Isaiah was the author of a large part of the book by that name. However, scholars believe that followers of Paul and followers of Isaiah wrote later works that were attributed to the better-known men. This was not dishonesty or carelessness. It could even be seen as a sign of respect for the greater prophet or preacher. Whatever the reason, attribution to a better known person was common and accepted in those times. People were less concerned about actual authorship than we are today.

For some books in the Bible, there is no one author. The first five books, the Pentateuch, traditionally attributed to Moses, might best be described as a collection of collections. They began as oral traditions, later written down by a number of unknown individuals in different areas. After several centuries, during which the Hebrew tribes had become one united people worshipping one God, other writers wove these separate traditions together to create the books as we know them.

The gospels also took shape gradually, though over a much shorter time span. At first, the Good News of Jesus Christ was preached. Then, as the people who had walked with Jesus began to die due to persecutions or old age, the church community saw a need to preserve the eyewitness accounts of the gospel. We know very little about the actual writers of the gospels, but we do know that a major goal was to faithfully transmit the gospel as it had been preached by the eyewitnesses. (See Lk 1:1–2, and Jn 21:24.)

It is important to say that our faith does not depend on the wisdom of the particular individuals who decided to write. None of these individuals wrote with the intention of putting their books in the Bible. It was a much more complicated process, concluding long after the authors were dead. For example, Paul wrote letters to the church communities where he had preached and established churches. We don't know how many letters he wrote. We do know that the communities saved some of his letters and used them for prayer and study because they recognized God's truth being preached to them in those writings. Those letters were saved, copied, and circulated among other church communities for generations before they were formally decreed to be part of the Bible.

In a real sense, the Bible is authored by the whole believing community. No writing was included in the Bible without widespread acceptance by the community, who first passed judgment by using and saving those writings that they found helpful to their growth in faith. So only those books which survived years of prayerful scrutiny by believers had a chance of being chosen for the Bible. The Christian Bible was put into final form two to three hundred years after the New Testament writing took place. The Christian church gave formal approval to the books still in our Bible today, rejecting many other books which were less widely used, or seemed less faithful to the gospel message, or maybe were just unnecessary. Most of those other writings were lost for centuries, though now we have found pieces of many of them. One of the best known is the "Gospel according to Thomas," which may have been rejected because of unacceptable elements such as magical stories about Jesus as a child.

As believers, we put our trust in the Holy Spirit. We believe that the Holy Spirit has guided the church at all stages, through the multitude of mostly unnamed believers who prayerfully preached, wrote, edited, selected, approved, and continue to translate and interpret God's word for us. The Bible does not stand alone; it is a very special written witness of the witnessing community. And in a sense, we can only trust in the Bible if we can trust in God's presence in the believing community that gives it to us. (Note: This is the Catholic view. Some Protestant denominations see the Bible as having an independent authority, greater than that of the community.)

Discussion Questions:

• How do I answer the question "Is everything in the Bible true?"
• How do I deal with the seeming differences between the Bible and scientific teaching?
• Have I been aware of God's word speaking to me in the Bible? Have I felt that any of my beliefs or assumptions have been challenged by the Bible?
• What attitudes or beliefs of our culture make it difficult for me to hear God's word?
• What other questions does this chapter raise for me?

Suggested Reading:

The New American Bible with Revised New Testament, The New Testament, "Preface to the First Edition" and "Preface to the Revised Edition"; also the introductory materials for any book you wish to study more closely.

Raymond E. Brown, *Responses to 101 Questions on the Bible* (Mahwah, NJ: Paulist Press, 1990). Very readable question and answer format. Brown is a well-known and respected Catholic theologian who has given innumerable lectures on the Bible.

Raymond E. Brown, S.S., *An Introduction to the New Testament* (New York/London/Toronto/Sydney/Auckland: Doubleday, 1997). For the truly enterprising, this major work will be a widely used reference for years to come. It is almost 900 pages, and gives a thorough review of the current scholarship on each New Testament book.

CHAPTER FOUR

The Bible
Understanding Writing Style and Purpose

Contents

This chapter will look at literary criticism of the biblical writings. What can we learn about the meaning of these writings, based on our knowledge of the writers, the situations in which the authors were writing, the literary styles used, and other information?

To find God's word in the Bible, we need to distinguish God's truth from the writing itself, which is the humanly created form in which God's message is presented. To discern the author's message, we need some knowledge of the literary forms used by the ancient writers. It also helps if we remind ourselves that, whatever the story, the author's primary goal is always to announce God's truth, not to give facts about history, science, or some other area of study.

Literary Forms: It's All True, and Some of It Is Myth

One important tool for understanding the Bible is literary criticism: discovering the form of literature the author was using. (Again, a good study Bible will give some background in the introduction at the beginning of each book.) Today we recognize that biblical authors used a variety of literary forms to announce God's truth. The Jewish people saw their own history as a powerful revelation of God's loving kindness, so they included much of their history in their Scripture. Some writers used poetry, songs, or stories. Some parts of the Bible contain a lot of factual material. Some parts, such as the creation stories or the Book of Revelation, contain very little that is literal fact.

One way to grasp this concept of message versus story form is to start with a familiar story, such as "The Hare and the Tortoise," from *Aesop's Fables*. I often begin discussion of this topic by asking "Is the story of 'The Hare and the Tortoise' true?" "Is it a lie?" And, "If it's not true, why do we keep telling the story, misleading innocent children?" Most people, including older children, are able to quickly clarify that the story is not literally true, but that it does teach a true message, which is why we keep using the story. It is not a lie because the purpose of a lie is to mislead someone. The goal of this story is to teach a truth, not to confuse. Children quickly figure out what part to believe when they are old enough. The story was never meant to be taken literally by anyone over the age of five. The truth it teaches—that talent alone is worth little, but perseverance will get you places—could be stated without the fanciful story. However, stories are much more memorable than lectures and easily understood. That is why stories have been more widely used throughout history. This is an example of the literary form called "myth." Myth—using the word in its literary sense—is not false; the message is some important truth, even though the story is not literal fact. (Unfortunately, in the popular use of the word, myth has come to mean "untruth.")

Many stories in the Bible are like "The Hare and the Tortoise." At first they may be taken literally; then, as we learn more about science and history, we conclude that some of these stories could not have actually happened. However, we still value the stories for the great truths they teach.

The story of Adam and Eve reveals profound truths about human beings, about our relationship to God, to others, and to the created world. Those messages are valid whether you think of Adam as an actual first human, or see him as a symbol for humankind. The biblical creation stories actually fit amazingly well with our modern knowledge of the evolution of the earth and living things. Adam was molded "out of the clay of the ground" (Gn 2:7). Modern science explains that life was formed slowly from "primordial soup," the stuff of the earth, through the process of evolution. Both Scripture and science tell us that we are part of the earth—creatures, not visiting gods. Both science and the Bible show our intimate connection with the rest of creation, our dependence on our environment and our responsibility for it. Modern scientists study chromosomes and mitochondria, and tell us we are all brothers and sisters, children of the same parents in the distant past.

Scientists have even used the same symbol, referring to an unknown female called "Eve," to whom all people on earth can trace ancestry. God revealed this truth thousands of years ago by inspiring wise and thoughtful people to intuitively put the same basic ideas in the Bible long before there was any formal proof from the study of science.

We do not look to the Bible to give us the factual details. The Bible tells us who created us and why we were created; science tells us how. If anything, the "why" is the more important question!

Creation and Evolution

The Christian debate over taking the Bible literally has most often focused on the creation stories. Did evolution just happen by accident, or did God create us through a loving, well-ordered plan? Are we just intelligent apes? Doesn't that destroy our dignity as human beings? Many Christians seem to find the theory of evolution a threat to faith. (It remains technically a theory, because scientific method requires that we do it again to prove it; the pope himself recently described evolution as "more than a hypothesis" today. See "Message to the Pontifical Academy of Sciences," December 5, 1996.)

There is no inherent conflict between religious faith and science. They are two entirely different kinds of knowledge that actually support each other. We can recognize God as the creator while understanding evolution as the awesome and complex mechanism through which God created life. This view is not only more believable, since the physical evidence is so overwhelming, but also more awe-inspiring than the simpler story of man fashioned from mud. Does it take away from our special status? Science affirms the importance of human decisions affecting all life on the earth, echoing the biblical proclamation that we have a very special status as co-creators or stewards, sharing God's dominion over creation. Again, the Bible addresses the big picture, pointing out our responsibility as caretakers of God's creation; science discovers the details of how our decisions are affecting the earth and other forms of life, and provides the practical information we need to work out responsible solutions. Science can help us understand how to be good stewards of God's creation.

Does evolution contradict the Bible? Let us look at the evidence from Scripture itself. The creation stories are recognized today as myth, made-up stories designed to teach some great truth. There is internal evidence that they were never meant to be taken literally. For example, there are two versions of the creation stories, and events happen in a different order in each version. In Genesis 1, humans were the last creation, the crowning event, on the last day of creation. In Genesis 2, man, but not yet woman, was created before any plants or animals. Then God decided that man needed a companion and created animals one by one. No animal was a suitable companion for Adam, so God created Eve out of Adam's rib.

What are we supposed to believe? Since the details, such as the order of events, do not agree, they are not part of the truth. Those details are not God's message to us, they are just the story form, which in this case is myth. Those story details are words of men, not the word of God. The ancient Jewish religious leaders included both stories with their conflicting details because together they reveal more of the will of God than either version reveals alone. Even though the details of the stories are different, the messages of the stories are consistent and complete each other. For example, in the first creation story humankind is created in the image and likeness of God, both male and female. This implies an equal dignity for men and women, but the idea is not developed further. In the second creation story, in which Eve is formed from Adam's rib, there is a direct focus on the relationship between men and women. Women are not like the animals, to be treated as property. They are to be intimate partners with men, not above or below but beside them. This is a revelation Christians and Jews are still struggling to fully understand.

Sometimes we note that certain biblical stories, particularly the creation and flood stories, are very similar to stories of other religions and cultures. To tell of God's actions before human memory, biblical storytellers and writers often borrowed ancient myths they had inherited from earlier times. But they took these existing stories and transformed them in the retelling so as to reveal a new understanding about God. This is a bit like taking the stones from an old, unwanted building and reusing the stones to construct a new and better structure, something ancient people frequently did. Some elements of the stories in the Bible are "old building material" reused to tell a new story with a profoundly new message. However this process occasionally left some odd "stones" laying around; there are a few passages that modern believers find disturbing, such as Genesis 6:1–4, which speaks of "sons of heaven" marrying "daughters of earth." These are just stray old stones that weren't cleaned out from the building site. We remind ourselves again that details of the story often should not be taken literally, and that the authors' limitations should not distract us from the religious teaching of a book, which is the message and the part which is true.

The biblical stories did use many elements that were old, but what made them different was that the message was new. The biblical creation stories tell us that God is a good God, and lord of all creation. They tell us that this good God created all things according to a deliberate plan, that all of creation is good, and that God intends for us to be happy. We are even called to a role of special dignity; we are to mirror God's glory by sharing in God's responsible care of creation and by showing God's kind of loving care for each other.

These messages are a wonderful revelation, in sharp contrast to the picture presented by the creation stories of neighboring Babylon, in which the gods were violent, people were created by accident from a slain god's blood, and the gods treated humans as slaves. The biblical stories, though similar in form, reveal a new and wonderfully empowering message: that God loves us, wants our happiness, and calls us to greatness. This is God's Word, God's Truth, presented through the words of men and women.

Recording History vs. Announcing the Good News

To understand any writing it helps to have a clear sense of the author's goals. The Bible was put together with the goal of announcing God's truth. The word "gospel" means "good news." We have four versions of the Good News of Jesus Christ. It is not a life of Jesus; it is not a history. The gospels have very little biographical material in them. The gospel preachers and writers were announcing the good news, the meaning of Jesus' ministry and death. They obviously were not trying to give us a biography. During that first generation, while the people who had known Jesus were still around, they could have put in more personal and historical detail if they had wanted to. Any proper biography would tell what a person looked like, their personal quirks and tastes, and details about all the years of the person's life. The evangelists obviously did not consider any of that important.

The well-loved infancy stories are probably more myth than history. The infancy stories were written to tell us who Jesus is for us. The stories proclaim Jesus' birth to be the result of the direct action of God; Jesus is clearly God's chosen one. His birth in the city of King David identifies Jesus with Jewish hopes for a new king who would reestablish the Jewish people as God's kingdom. But there are also predictions of his death; Jesus is a different kind of savior who will not glory in earthly power and wealth but instead is destined to die for us. The gifts of the three wise men include gold, symbolizing kingship, and myrrh, symbolizing suffering. (It is worth noting that the gospels were written well after the death of Jesus. The Christian community had spent a generation figuring our how to announce the good news, the meaning of Jesus, before these books were written.)

The infancy stories are very meaningful but probably not very historical. Some of the most compelling evidence for that conclusion is the evidence within Scripture itself. First, only two of the four gospels contain infancy stories, and those two sets in Matthew and Luke are almost completely different from one another. It is difficult to reconcile them if one tries to take them as literal history. For example, in Matthew's gospel, Mary and Joseph appear to live in Bethlehem, and it is only after their sojourn in Egypt that they move to Nazareth. (See Mt 2:21–23.) In Luke, Mary and Joseph are from Nazareth, and they go to Bethlehem because of the census. (See Lk 2:1–5.) There is no mention of Egypt at all. What are the common elements in these two stories? They both identify Jesus as the man historically known to be from Nazareth, and they both affirm his identity as the Messiah by placing his birth in Bethlehem, city of the great King David. In other words, they both say that Jesus is the real historical man from Nazareth and that he is God's chosen Messiah. These parts of the two versions match, and they are the important parts! However, the warm human stories make the infancy narratives all the more compelling and memorable.

Another clue is that there is a marked discontinuity between the infancy stories and the ministry stories. For example, in the infancy stories, many people recognize Jesus as a very special baby, a king or savior. But when we read of Jesus' ministry, there is no evidence that anyone remembers a special birth. In fact, we have passages in which people question the importance of Jesus by saying in essence, "Isn't this just the kid who grew up down the street?" (See Mt 13:54–57). They didn't remember anything unusual about his past. If his family had moved to the town when he was a child, that, too, would have been noted; he would still have been considered a newcomer.

This lack of knowledge about a special or unusual birth is very evident in Mark's gospel, which has no infancy stories at all. (So Mark, as the author, had no need to try to reconcile ministry stories with infancy.) Mark's gospel is believed to be the earliest, and is in many ways the most "down to earth" version of the Jesus story. We get the most human portrayal of Jesus in Mark. Jesus becomes tired, hungry, and frustrated with the continued confusion of his disciples. (See Mk 8:17–21.) We also have the clearest picture of what people understood about Jesus at the time he was preaching. The later gospel writers put far more post-resurrection faith in the mouths of people. In other words, in later versions of the gospel, people make more statements that could not have been made before the resurrection actually happened. The infancy stories are the most blatant examples of this, but in the ministry narratives we occasionally have someone announcing that Jesus is the Son of God (Mt 16:16). That is a statement of the church's faith as it developed later on, not something anyone would have said during Jesus' earthly life.

What did the disciples really know during the years when they were listening to Jesus preach? The story of the disciples on the road to Emmaus after Jesus has died (Lk 24:13–35) is a very good clue. The disciples say they had been "hoping that he would be the one to redeem Israel" (verse 21), but obviously, their hopes had been dashed by his death. In other words, they had not understood beforehand that he was to be a suffering servant who would die for us. It is only later, "in the breaking of the bread"—the celebration of the Mass—that they recognize the risen Jesus with them. It is only after prayerful reflection on the life and death of Jesus that the followers recognize that the risen Jesus lives and is still with us. But then this post-resurrection awareness was written into the gospel stories as though people had known it during Jesus' lifetime. This kind of writing was entirely acceptable at that time. The writers were telling us the good news, who Jesus is for us, not factual history as we would expect in a modern news report.

The last gospel written is the gospel of John, which very strongly emphasizes the divinity of Jesus; so much so that it is hard to see Jesus as a real human being. That is why the church preserved four gospels. Each gospel presents some parts of the Christian belief particularly well, together they give us a more complete gospel. None of them are strictly historical; their purpose is to tell the Good News, not names and dates like a newspaper report.

We citizens of the twenty-first century like to know what is historical fact. In the gospels, the narratives about the passion and death of Jesus appear to be the earliest and most historical parts of the Jesus material. Then gradually the ministry accounts took shape as a collection of separate stories and sayings. The four evangelists, the gospel writers, strung these stories and sayings together into four different, clearly artificial sequences of events—like four people putting loose beads on a string, creating four different beautiful neck-laces. The first three gospel writers used many of the same stories. Books are available that print the sections of these three gospels in parallel columns, which makes it easy to see how the same story has been used in a different con-text by each writer. For example, the parable of the sower is in chapter 13 of Matthew, chapter 4 in Mark, and 8 in Luke. The last gospel materials to take shape were the infancy stories of Matthew and Luke. The two sets of infancy stories create far too many historical problems and are judged to be the least historical part of the gospels. As noted earlier the two sets are almost totally different stories—with the same message, of course. They make more sense when understood as post-resurrection faith expressed in vivid story form.

Large parts of the Hebrew Scriptures, our Old Testament, are historical material, but again we must remember that the author's purpose was not to record historical facts. Sometimes the story of the Jewish people is called sal-vation history, meaning that it is really about the history of God's saving relationship with the people. Sometimes it is called religiously interpreted history, emphasizing that the historical facts have been selected, interpreted, and even sometimes rearranged to tell the real story, the story about God. We have to respect the attitude of the biblical writers, who worked within the accepted thinking of their times. The authors felt free to use and reshape his-torical details in order to clarify the message about God, which was the pur-pose of their writing.

Today we are inclined to be offended at inaccuracy in the way facts are recorded. We come from a newspaper and video culture, and we expect that news people have precisely recorded "who, what, when, and where." The Bible was composed and written at a time when most people could not write.

People depended on oral accounts of events. They did not expect all the facts. Lacking tape recorders, it was understood that authors reconstructed conversations, always with the goal of revealing the significance of events, answering the questions "why and what does it mean for us?" On the other hand, oral cultures can be very good at preserving the facts when they consider them important, and recent archaeological work has verified the historical nature of many biblical names and events.

Discussion Questions:

• Does literary criticism make it easier or harder to believe in the Bible as God's word?

• Is biblical literalism or fundamentalism an issue in local schools? If so, what is happening to education and to faith as a result?

• Are there parts of the Bible that make you uncomfortable because you don't know whether to take them literally or not?

CHAPTER FIVE

Biblical Prophets and Predictions

Contents

This chapter will look at prophets and predictions, and in particular at the Book of Revelation, because these topics are very popular. However, they are also generally misunderstood.

Prophets and Predictions

What is a prophet? In our popular culture, a prophet is often assumed to be someone who can predict the future, much as a fortune teller or psychic is believed to do. This is not the biblical understanding of a prophet.

In the Bible prophets are understood to be good and prayerful individuals called by God to speak God's word forcefully to the people. Sometimes, when the people were suffering exile or oppression, the prophet's message was a gentle reassurance that God would not abandon them. In the centuries before Jesus, the Jews had interpreted this promise as a promise of independence and prosperity in their own land, where they could worship without outside interference and be the people God called them to be. This was the reason they had to be freed from Egypt, because Pharaoh did not allow them the time and freedom to worship. (See Ex 5:1.)

Often, though, the prophet's message was a warning that the people were straying from their covenant relationship with God and not keeping God's life-giving commands. Then the prophet's message would include some warning of the consequences of a sinful society; they would not be strong, and their enemies would conquer them.

The prophets did not have any secret knowledge of events in the future. What they did know was that God is a good God, who wants us to build a peaceful and just society for all people. They also knew that sin is destructive and tears society apart, and that a state weakened from within is vulnerable to attack. From that combination of faith and practical wisdom, they concluded that the current enemy, whoever that might be, would become the tool of punishment if the people failed to follow God's life-giving ways.

There is a further interesting note on the subject of predicting the future. In the gospels, Jesus indicates that even he does not know when the world will end (Mk 13:32). Jesus is a human being, and experienced life as a human being. He knew what a human could know, and no human being—not a prophet or even Jesus—can predict such things. Prophets do not have secret knowledge; they are prayerful, thoughtful people who see the truth revealed in life and announce it boldly, without watering it down to be politically wise or to tell people what they want to hear. (As a consequence, many of the prophets, and of course Jesus, were treated badly by people who did not want the status quo challenged.)

The above explanations assume that God works through the natural order and through the natural talents of people. Most modern Scripture scholars reflect the scientific assumptions of our day, that all events in biblical times were as natural as the world we know now. They tend to assume that events in biblical times could theoretically have been explained in scientific terms, if a modern scientist had been there to get the facts. Today we can reconstruct natural explanations for some events, such as the crossing of the Red Sea. For many stories, however, we don't have enough information. That was not the biblical author's goal or way of seeing reality. (More on this in chapter 10, on miracles.)

To look at it another way, many people today believe that God's power and presence are seen through this marvelous creation, rather than by suspending the natural order that God has so wondrously fashioned. With eyes of faith, all of nature is awesome revelation. This actually gets closer to the biblical way of thinking. What we think of as the traditional distinction between natural and supernatural is not biblical. It is a later European way of viewing reality. Biblical writers wrote with the pre-scientific assumption of their times that God directly controlled all events, so God could be seen in all things. When the weather was good for crops, they saw it as God's blessing; when disaster struck, they often saw it as a punishment for their sins.

But even the Bible warns against too simple an interpretation. The disciples asked Jesus if a man's blindness was punishment for the man's sins or punishment for his parents' sins, since the man had been born that way. Jesus answered that the blindness was not punishment for anyone's sin, but "it is so that the works of God might be made visible through him" (Jn 9:1–3). Believers today can see the evidence of God's loving care through all of creation, just as the biblical writers did, without interpreting each event as a direct reward or punishment.

The Book of Revelation

Whenever people are asked what biblical topics they would like to study, questions always surface about the Book of Revelation, also called the Revelation to John, or the Apocalypse. The book is very popular but also very misunderstood. It is fascinating because it appears to make predictions, and we would all like to know what is going to happen in the future. We should first remind ourselves that the only kind of predictions found in the Bible are predictions born of faith. There are no predictions revealing secret knowledge. That is simply not the belief shown us in the Bible.

The Book of Revelation is a form of literature not familiar to us from our own literary culture. It is called apocalyptic literature, which is why the book is often called the Apocalypse. The Book of Daniel and Mark 13 are other examples of apocalyptic literature in the Bible.

Some scholars explain apocalyptic literature as a form of resistance literature: a veiled form of writing that seems to have been used during times of oppression. In a sense, it is coded: "Wisdom is needed here; one who understands can calculate" (Rv 13:18). It is full of symbolism that the Jews (the insiders) would have understood, but foreigners, such as their Greek or Roman overlords, would not have understood. This made it possible for the Jews and early Christians to use this symbolism to make the faith statement that God would not let the oppression last; God would free them and destroy the power of Rome. It encouraged Christians to keep the faith and

BIBLICAL NUMBER SYMBOLISM

1000 means

"an immense number."

12 means

12 tribes, the whole Jewish people, or 12 apostles, the whole Christian church; common meaning, "the whole people of God."

10 means

an indefinite round number, like saying "a bunch of people." It is a significant bunch, though; enough to matter, not just a random one or two. In the Jewish tradition, ten men were required to form a synagogue.

7 means

"complete, whole, or good" (probably took on that meaning because people were using a 7-day weekly calendar.) Note: Christians have used this same symbolism by creating many lists of seven things for people to memorize. This was both symbolic and a practical memory aid: If you remembered seven you knew you had them all, and the list of seven had that larger meaning of totality. For example, the seven sacraments celebrate all the many ways Christian life is sacramental.

6 means

"incomplete, evil" (because it falls short of 7!)

3 means

"emphasis" or indicates "time of fulfillment" when things happen. (Peter denied Jesus three times. In other words, he really did choose to deny Jesus; this was not a momentary slip of the tongue. The resurrection, like many events, happens "on the third day.")

stand firm against the evil empire in spite of the persecution they were suffering. It might not have been safe to say such things openly. Instead, the Book of Revelation speaks of the "harlot Babylon" which represents Rome (see Rv 17). But if a Roman soldier had happened to see the book, he would probably have laughed at it and considered it silly nonsense. He would not have recognized the subversive message.

The most important thing to remember about the Book of Revelation is that almost nothing in it should be taken literally. It is full of symbols. The colors, objects, numbers, and outlandish beasts each represent something else. In the past century, Scripture scholars have come to understand much of the symbolism. For example, numbers are almost always symbolic. The same number symbolism is used throughout the Bible; it is not unique to this book, but this book is especially dominated by symbolism.

Combining numbers combines meanings. The number 666 combines 6 and 3, meaning evil emphasized, that is, very, very evil. In Rv 13:18, this number is believed to refer to Nero and the other Roman emperors who were persecuting God's church. Another frequently quoted number is 144,000, the number of "servants of God" mentioned in a vision in Rv 7. Some fundamentalist Christians have taken this to be the literal number of people to be saved, though verses 9–17 recount another vision of a great multitude "which no one could count" from every race and nation who are clearly to be saved. What symbol can we find in 144,000? We get that number by multiplying 12 x 12 x 1000. It combines the meaning of 12, the whole people of God, with 1000, an immense number. Clearly this is not meant as an exact count of anything, but as a faith statement that an immense number of God's faithful people will be saved. Perhaps it is even an immense number of God's faithful people of both the old and the new covenant (twelve tribes and twelve apostles).

The passage about the 144,000 also has another symbol. The 144,000 are called "Israelites" which, if we took it literally, would exclude most Christians since few of us are Jews. (Fundamentalist Christians who take the 144,000 as a literal count don't take "Israelites" literally.) Christian symbolism often compares the church to the Jewish tribes. The church, symbolized by 12 apostles, is the new people of God just as the 12 tribes were the first people of God. So "Israelites" often means Christians, again reminding us that almost nothing in this book is to be taken literally. It is a deeply meaningful statement of faith that God will save the people of all nations who have remained faithful through persecution. It is a message of hope to Christians whose faith might be shaken by hard times.

The Book of Revelation gives us a message we still need to hear when it seems as though the world rewards wrongdoing, and we wonder if it's worth trying to do what is right. We wonder if God really cares or really exists, and we are assured that all will be set right in God's time; we need to keep up hope. Evil may sometimes seem invincible, like some sort of raging beast, but we are assured that evil will not last; it will ultimately fall. Only good will last. The writer of the Book of Revelation communicates this Christian faith in the ultimate power of a good God who will in time claim all of creation for good. This is a fitting close for the Bible, which began by telling us that a good God created all things, and affirmed each creation with the words "God saw how good it was" (Gn 1). The author of the Book of Revelation does not have any inside knowledge of when the world will end, or any other secret knowledge. What he speaks is the faith of the church that God is in control, and that good will be rewarded.

Discussion Questions:
• Does the Book of Revelation offer us anything helpful to our faith today?
• Do you think there are prophets in the world today? How can we tell who is a prophet?
• Have you ever felt that God wanted you to speak out about something?

Suggested Reading:
David P. Reid, SS. CC., *What Are They Saying about the Prophets?* (Mahwah, NJ: Paulist Press, 1980). Short, under 100 pages, but fairly academic in tone. This book is a holistic view of prophecy, not a history of individual books and prophets.

CHAPTER SIX

Father, Son, and Spirit

Contents

This chapter will attempt to give a brief explanation of the concept of the Trinity, closing with an updated version of St. Patrick's well-known explanation. Be sure to read the last paragraph, even if the rest of the chapter is confusing!

The Trinity is a basic Christian doctrine, one of the beliefs that were formally defined, mostly in the fourth century, to clarify church belief and weed out what was seen as heresy. Most Catholics will say they believe the doctrine of the Trinity, they just are not sure what it really means!

Reading theology books on this subject can be very frustrating. Theologians repeatedly remind us that all language about God is insufficient because God is beyond us. All language about God is also symbolic because we think and speak in terms of the world we know; again, God the creator is beyond the created world of which we are a part. Another way to say this is that all language about God is from a "human's-eye view." In other words, it is a description of how we perceive or experience God. We cannot define or explain God from an objective position, like the scientist observing something in a test tube; we cannot observe God from above or outside of God. In technical terms, a theologian might say the doctrine is best understood as existential, an expression of our experience, more than ontological, an explanation of God's being. Unfortunately, I think our western European culture tends to read everything as though it is meant to be a scientist's objective observation.

Lastly, we are struggling to understand a concept defined in a different age and culture. The traditional definition of "three persons in one God" is misleading today because the concept of persons is quite different today from what the word meant centuries ago. We think of persons as unique thinking, experiencing beings, completely separate from and different from other unique beings, and unable to ever completely understand other persons. This is not what we mean by the three persons in one God because that would negate the oneness of God.

Theologians struggle to find words to talk about God, sometimes speaking of a God who is Being. This God Being is always active and always Being-in-relation, a God who is Love. Love is not something static; it is a verb. It is an action of going out to others. The doctrine of the Trinity is saying that this creative "going out to others" is a constant reality in God, inherent in Being's self; and so the three persons are constantly in relationship.

But while recognizing the limitations of our language and of our knowledge of God, the doctrine of the Trinity expresses a very important tradition about the human experience of God. Even though the doctrine was not formally defined until well after the writing of the Bible, we can say that trinitarian belief is found in Scripture, particularly in the Christian writings. The New Testament identifies Jesus with the Word God expressed, the second person of the Trinity. The Prologue to John's gospel, which was probably an early church hymn, clearly expresses both the separateness and the unity of Father and Son, and expresses them as an eternal relationship; something about God that always was, even before Jesus of Nazareth was born. "In the beginning was the Word, and the Word was with God, and the Word was God....And the Word became flesh" (Jn 1:1, 14). The Bible also describes the Spirit, God unifying and empowering us from within. This Spirit is called the Holy Spirit, the Spirit of God, and Jesus sometimes refers to "my spirit," clearly all the same Spirit.

Taking an experience-centered approach, we can say that in Scripture we find that the one God has been encountered three different ways, and that this God is always encountered as person. God is encountered as Father/Creator, the image that dominates the earliest Scriptures. God is the creator and provider of all; the life-giver, the source of order, the one who nurtures life. This is the dominant view of God in the Old Testament. This God is generally experienced as Other; distant, inscrutable, inspiring awe and fear. In Jesus, a fellow human, Christians have encountered God as God expressed, the spoken Word made present to us in a very concrete way, Emmanuel, God with us. But after the resurrection, the followers of Jesus were lost; they had no direction. Then in Acts, we see the followers of Jesus who discover the Spirit present and active through them, the church community. The church is the people who are conscious of the power of God alive within them, making them the continued body of Christ on earth. This presence of the Spirit of God was symbolized by the "tongues as of fire" ("as of"—in other words, not real fire) in the story of Pentecost in Acts 2:3. It is the same lively symbol seen in the book of Exodus. The burning bush was not consumed because it wasn't real fire, either. In the book of Exodus we also find fire, the pillar of fire (a pillar of fire by night, smoke by day: Ex 13:21)

At the same time, the Christian doctrine of the Trinity is saying that this is more than just three ways of seeing the one God. It is three expressions of God's being, three expressions who exist constantly and are constantly in relation. But that takes us back toward a philosophical definition rather than experience.

Years ago, while trying to explain the Trinity, I recalled the shamrock, the symbol St. Patrick used to explain the Trinity. I had seen the shamrock many times, three leaves on one stem used to symbolize three persons in one God. This symbol had never really clarified anything for me. Suddenly I saw something that had never struck me before. In effect, I discovered a new natural symbol for the Trinity that worked better for me than the old symbol did. Drawing from biology, I realized that any part of the shamrock, a leaf or even one cell, contains the full genetic code; everything that a shamrock is or can be is contained in that one cell. Patrick was saying the same thing. He was saying that any part of the shamrock contained the full shamrock nature. My knowledge of biology helped me understand what Patrick was trying to say—that whether we encounter God as Father/Creator, as the Son Jesus, or as the enlivening Spirit moving within people, it is the same one-and-only-one God, the same divine nature, fully present in those three expressions or three persons.

Discussion Questions:

• How does the teaching about the Trinity help us understand God?

• How does the teaching about the Trinity help us understand ourselves?

• Was there anything in this chapter that was new to you or confusing?

Suggested Reading:

William L. Portier, *Tradition & Incarnation: Foundations of Christian Theology* (Mahwah, NJ: Paulist Press, 1994). An introductory college text addressing our Christian beliefs about Jesus. Fundamental theology that does not lose a spirit of faith and celebration of our tradition.

CHAPTER SEVEN

Jesus
Fully God and Fully Human

Contents

This chapter will review the doctrine of the Incarnation, the essential Christian teaching that Jesus is true man and true God, and will consider several symbols and images used to try to communicate this idea. Then there is a close examination of what we believe about human nature and what we believe about divine nature, so that we can better grasp the teaching that the two natures come together in Jesus.

The Incarnation is a fundamental concept central to Christian belief: that Jesus is God in human flesh, fully God and at the same time fully human. We Christians have always found it difficult to put these two ideas together in our heads. In fact, several centuries passed before the belief was clearly defined, and alternative explanations of Jesus' nature were rejected and defined as heresy. For two thousand years believers have struggled with this belief, often slipping into one or another of the early heresies, either denying that Jesus is truly human or denying that he is truly God. Today there are still many people who know Jesus was a real human being but don't quite know what we mean by saying he is also God. For a long time, however, including more than half of the twentieth century, most Christians were very certain that Jesus is God but not convinced that he really experienced human life as we know it, with all of its uncertainty, temptations, and limits. For some people, human and God are like oil and water; they just don't mix. (This means oil and water are not good symbols for us to use in this case!)

Let us begin by addressing the issue of symbols. We are constantly using symbols in our everyday language. Symbolic expressions are shortcuts to help us communicate a lot in a few words. If I say, "Sue is sweet," I am reminding you of the taste of sweet foods, and suggesting that Sue has an equally pleasing personality. We use lots of symbols for God, whom we cannot see. We call God "Father," reminding ourselves of the loving care and attention a good father shows for his children. Michelangelo painted a wonderful picture on the Sistine Chapel ceiling of God creating Adam. God is portrayed as a physically vigorous but mature gray-haired man, reaching out from a posture that communicates power. The artist undoubtedly wanted us to see God as masterful and strong, with the wisdom we associate with maturity. But symbols can also suggest things we don't want to communicate. Today people look at traditional European art and realize that it also seems to assume that God is white and male, even though our theology clearly says God is pure spirit, without a body, race, or gender. (Jesus, of course, had a specific human body, male and Semitic.) The point is, symbols can both clarify and confuse the message.

If we are subconsciously using the wrong images, such as oil and water for God and human, we won't be able to see the true message. We will end up with some idea of Jesus as partly God and partly man. However, that is not Christian belief. Many ancient people, such as the Greeks, did believe in demigods: beings that were half god, half human, not really either, with some of the characteristics of each. They could be imaged as oil and water, a half-and-half image, or as milk and water, which would result in something which is neither one nor the other but something in between. Instead, Christians proclaim that Jesus is as human as you or I and at the same time equal in divinity with the Father. How can we image that? Let us first go back to the Bible to reaffirm the faith stated there.

The Bible makes it evident that the followers of Jesus first knew him as an ordinary human being. Then, through his preaching, miracles, and the witness of his life and death, they made a leap of faith to declare that this man Jesus was the Son of God, the Messiah of Jewish hopes, the Savior of all humankind.

The Gospel Proclamation: Jesus as Man

The belief that Jesus is fully God and fully human is clearly presented in Scripture. The gospels identify Jesus as a real historical person. He was a man from Nazareth, known as a carpenter, the son of Joseph and Mary. Independent historical sources also verify his historical existence. His life in his home town was so ordinary that when Jesus became known for working miracles, his old neighbors, who obviously just remembered him as the kid who grew up down the street, thought he was putting on airs (Mt 13:54–58). The Gospel according to Mark also portrays a Jesus who gets tired and hungry and frustrated with the slowness of his disciples (Mk 8:17–21). Jesus feels the very human temptation to avoid suffering. He needs to withdraw to a quiet place to pray and prepare for challenges. He cries out in pain and faith from the cross, reciting Psalm 22 (Mk 15:34). The Jesus portrayed in the gospels is clearly a man who experienced the frustrations, hurts, temptations, and fears of human life. This Jesus is a fellow human being with whom we can feel kinship. St. Paul calls him the "firstborn of many brothers" (Rm 8:29). (Paul's words might better be translated "brothers and sisters." Paul is speaking of that common human bond Jesus has with all of us.)

The Gospel Proclamation: Jesus as God

The gospels also clearly affirm the Christian belief that this man Jesus is God. The beginning of the Gospel according to John, probably drawing from an already existing Christian hymn, proclaims: "In the beginning was the Word, and the Word was with God, and the Word was God.... And the Word became flesh" (Jn 1:1,14) and "No one has ever seen God. The only Son, God, who is at the Father's side, has revealed him" (Jn 1:18).

If the followers of Jesus first knew him as a human being, how did they come to the point of proclaiming him God? There were two Jewish concepts that helped the first Christians make that leap of faith. The first concept is the "word." The spoken word is a powerful concept in many cultures. The spoken word is an idea made concrete, made real, given life. The spoken word is active, it makes things happen. "Then God said 'Let there be light,' and there was light" (Gn 1:3). Christians proclaim that Jesus is the "Word of God made flesh," the power of the unseen God visibly, actively, concretely present in our human world.

A note for you...

Saturday, Sept 5, '09

Fr. Mike,

Attached is the book we will be using for our men's group meeting starting Monday, 9/14. We will be meeting at Bill Coffin's house at 720 Springlock Ave, Silver Spring, Md —
Phone - 301-625-7737

Dennis O'Malley

*A note
for you...*

Of course, Jesus' earthly life was long ago, and you and I were not there to see, hear, or touch Jesus in the flesh. But we have the historical memory of Jesus' earthly life. Gospel writers made a point of noting that they were transmitting the gospel as given by eyewitnesses (Lk 1:1–4) so that we might be confident of that nearness to the real historical Jesus too. We celebrate the continued real presence of Jesus in the flesh of his followers, the church community, through the Eucharist. (That is why it is so important to regularly participate in the Sunday Mass. It is the celebration of our identity as Christians, reminding us to be the visible, acting body of Christ in community.) So we continue to know Jesus as the Word made flesh among us, God in our midst.

A second important Jewish concept is the true son. In the centuries before writing was commonly used, if a patriarch or leader needed to send an important message, he told it to a messenger verbally and had to trust that the messenger would transmit the message accurately. A servant or a slave might not understand and might not care either. Only a true son, one who knew his father's mind and was loyal, could be counted on to faithfully and accurately communicate his father's will. To hear such a son was as good as hearing the father; in fact, it was hearing the father. It was more trustworthy than the signed and sealed documents of later centuries, which could be a fraud. The followers of Jesus came to recognize Jesus as the true son of God, who spoke and witnessed to the Father's message so faithfully that it was the same as hearing God. This meant Jesus was God made present in this human being. (The literal meaning of the word son refers to a biological relationship. Obviously, son is used here in a symbolic sense, since God is spirit.)

The Jewish Scriptures, the books of our Old Testament, express awe and respect for a God who is beyond human understanding. Moses was not allowed to approach God too closely (Ex 3:5–6). The Christian proclamation that our brother Jesus is God in our midst puts humankind in a new relationship with God. God is no longer distant on a high mountain; God is with us. We see this closeness again in the coming of the Spirit at Pentecost. The Spirit came in "tongues as of fire" resting on the heads of the believers. Now the distance between God and people has been completely eliminated, and there is no sense of fear at the approach of the almighty God. God and humankind have been joined; God is not only with us, God is within us.

But do we really grasp this teaching? Do we really understand that our brother Jesus, who knows the struggle and uncertainty of human life, is God in our midst, joining us all to God in a new way? This is one of those profound mysteries that bears further contemplation because even if we know it, we never fully grasp the significance. We can always continue to grow in our appreciation of its meaning.

Finding an Image that Works

People have tried to express the significance of Jesus through many symbols. Jesus is called a mediator, a bridge. Moses kept a respectful distance from a God who inspired awe and fear; God was Other, beyond us. Jesus bridges the gap; in him God and humankind are joined forever. And as brothers and sisters of Jesus, we now have a permanent mediator, a bridge forever joining the two sides in the person of Jesus, who is both God and human. We no longer need to feel that God is distant.

I came up with another image which many of my students found helpful in grasping the idea of Jesus as God and human. One day when I was teaching this topic, I was wearing a favorite turtleneck, a 100% cotton, vivid purple shirt. That shirt became my symbol. It is 100% cotton and also 100% purple, and the addition of the purple does not in any way dilute, water down, or change the nature of the cotton. It is still fully cotton, with all the same characteristics as any other comfortable cotton knit shirt. It is also as purple as purple can be.

This is what we are saying about Jesus. He is fully human, with the same human nature that you and I have. And he is also fully God, equal to the Father. Human nature is not in any way diluted by the divine nature. Human nature becomes a vehicle for the divine, in the same way that a cotton shirt becomes a vehicle for color, without the nature of the cotton being changed. The shirt loses nothing from its cotton characteristics, but the color transforms it into something more. Two realities coexist fully. They do not clash or compete, or work against each other in any way. Cotton is ideally suited to express color. Likewise, humans are ideally suited to express God. That is our biblical faith. Human beings are created to image God. Imaging God is not contrary to human nature. If we believe the Bible, imaging God is human nature. But I think we have a hard time believing that, because of our culture's beliefs about human nature. Our culture does not believe that humans are capable of imaging God. Our culture denigrates human nature, seeing it as inherently lowly: dirty, sinful, or depraved. Popular jokes, TV programs, and films mock human nature. We speak of sin and failure as "only human," as though that is all that is to be expected of human nature.

Human Nature: Image of God

God incarnate—in the flesh—was a new concept. Maybe I should say this is a new concept, because many Christians still find it puzzling. If it is hard to imagine what human nature coexisting with divine nature means, then possibly it will help to examine what we believe about human nature and what we believe about divine nature.

Returning to Scripture, we are told in Genesis that we are made "in the image and likeness of God" (Gn 1:26–27). What does this mean? It obviously does not mean we look like God, since God, being spirit, doesn't look like anything. But it does mean that our human nature is designed to reflect, and in some less complete sense, to be like the Creator. We Christians are saying something very similar when we say we are called to be other Christs. Is it easier to say "we are called to be Christ to each other," than "we are called to be like God"? But that is the same call. And that is precisely why Jesus is so important. We can understand the challenge to live as Jesus did because he is one of us. But Jesus is one with the Father/Creator, so to image Jesus is to image God. And to carry it one step further, to image Jesus is to image God is to be what we are called to be, the image and likeness of God. Ultimately, then, the biblical message is calling us to be true to ourselves!

It is worth belaboring this point a bit. Our popular culture often suggests that to be good is a denial of our human nature; that we have to deny basic human needs and feelings in order to be holy. Sex in particular is seen as less than holy. This is very bad theology. This negative view is not from the Bible, in which God created us male and female, and saw that it was good. It is from pagan Greek philosophy (which later resulted in heresies in the church) in which the rational mind was seen as good and the more emotional and physical side of human nature was seen as too animal-like and less dignified. Unfortunately, pagan Greek culture dominated the world of the early church, and this negative attitude towards God's creation crept into

Christian thinking. But as Christians, we need to remember that marriage, an actively sexual relationship, is celebrated as a sacrament, a sacred sign which is lived out daily and images God's love for humankind. A sacrament is an opportunity to encounter God. Nothing can be holier than a sacrament! There is no conflict between being human and acting in a God-like way. If we believe God's word in Genesis, to be God-like is a deeply human thing to do; it is the way to human fulfillment and happiness.

As brothers and sisters of Jesus, we are called to be other Christs and temples of the Holy Spirit. We are called to recognize the presence of God within us, empowering us to carry on the work of Jesus, as the early Christians did after Pentecost. The central theme in the Acts of the Apostles is the Spirit of God acting through the followers of Jesus, doing the work of healing, preaching, and witnessing, even witnessing through death, just as Jesus did. The church is conscious of the call to image Jesus, to be Jesus still present in the world. But according to the Bible, all people are called by their very nature to image God. Believers are only set apart in that we know it.

That brings us to the next logical question: how do we image God?

Divine Nature: God is a Verb

What portrait of God is seen in Scripture? God is never described visually. The Jewish (and Islamic) faith today continue the tradition of not allowing pictures of God because our pictures would inevitably be too small, too limited, a God made in our image (as is Michelangelo's white male God). In the Bible we see God in action. Even the symbols of God's presence are active elements: moving, powerful things, such as fire and wind, bespeaking a Power beyond human control. In other words, God is always encountered as an active force. In the Hebrew Scriptures, we see God creating, instructing, protecting, freeing, guiding, and disciplining (discipline being a positive act to bring the people back to God's life-giving ways). In Christian Scriptures, we see Jesus teaching, healing, forgiving, and giving life. God is God-in-action. Some years ago, banners proclaiming "God is Love" were very popular. Love is a verb. It is not some thing. It is not a warm feeling. It is a way to act. It is doing for others, "so that they might have life and have it more abundantly" (Jn 10:10). God is always encountered as an active, loving Power who is giving life and calling us to choose life in every possible way.

So back to our original question: How are we to image God? By loving as God loves because that is what God is. We are called to image God by imaging God's loving, life-giving action for others. Choose life. Love your neighbor as yourself. Love one another as I have loved you. This is not merely a command, it is our nature. We are most truly ourselves in loving others. Since this is what we were created for, it is our way to happiness, fulfillment, salvation.

Jesus Our Savior

This brings us back again to the special role of Jesus. It is precisely because Jesus is one of us that he is able to be our savior. Jesus is God, but we must not forget he is also human! He shows us the God of Love, but he also shows us how to be fully human. If the gospel were only about Jesus, it might be interesting but it would be irrelevant. The story about Jesus is good news because it is our story too. Paul makes this connection when he says, "For if the dead are not raised, neither has Christ been raised, and if Christ has not been raised, your faith is in vain"(1 Cor 15:16–17). The resurrection of Jesus is good news because it is the promise that we all shall rise as our brother Jesus did, in spite of life's pain, suffering, and loss. If we live as Jesus did, choosing to be life-givers, healers, forgivers, we will not be defeated by loss or even death; we will find fulfillment, resurrection, eternal life. To live as Jesus did would be a true celebration of biblical faith, faith in the God of Life, who calls us to choose life that we might live (Dt 30:15–16).

Discussion Questions:
• How does the life of Jesus help me understand God?
• How does the life of Jesus help me understand my own life?
• Are there images or symbols of God that I especially like? Images of Jesus?
• Are there images I don't like?

Suggested Readings:
William L. Portier, *Tradition & Incarnation: Foundations of Christian Theology* (Mahwah, NJ: Paulist Press, 1994). An introductory college textbook addressing our Christian beliefs about Jesus. Fundamental theology that does not lose a spirit of faith and celebration of our tradition.

CHAPTER EIGHT

The Cross and the Gospel of Life
(And a Reflection on Martyrdom)

Contents
This chapter reflects on the meaning of the death of Jesus, while adhering to the belief that God is always the God of life, Abba.

For many people the cross has been a stumbling block, getting in the way of their full acceptance of Christianity. In the first century, it was primarily the humiliation of a person being executed as a criminal that was hard to accept. The modern equivalent would be a Jesus who had been sent to the electric chair. We would recoil from that idea not only because it is barbaric, but because we generally presume that people who are executed really are guilty of some terrible wrong. (Though of course, there is plenty of evidence that this is not always true, today or in the time of Jesus!)

Today people ask more often what the crucifixion says about our belief in God. Why did Jesus have to die? Or did he? How can a God of love also be a vengeful God who demands the suffering of his son? And in what way are we saved by the death of Jesus?

The gospels proclaim a Jesus who came so that we might have life. Everything Jesus did—healing, forgiving, teaching—was to bring people to the fullest experience of life. And everything that Jesus does echoes the God portrayed in the Jewish Scriptures that Jesus himself read. The Scriptures Jesus read, our Old Testament books, tell of a God who creates, provides all good things, forgives, liberates, guides, and calls his people to "choose life." Jesus called this God "Abba," "Father"; someone who would not hand his child a stone when the child asked for bread (Mt 7:7–11). Yet somehow we ended up with a popular image of a God who demanded retribution, a blood payment for the sin of humankind.

The interpretation of the death of Jesus as a debt paid for sin is found in the Bible. When the focus is on why Jesus was willing to face death, it makes sense and does not offend our faith. It makes sense to say that Jesus was motivated by his love for us, and because of that was willing to pay a personal price to free us from the darkness and confusion of sin. But to portray God the Father as a vengeful ruler who demands blood because his power and dignity have been challenged or insulted is offensive. That is not the father Jesus portrayed in his parables. It is contrary to the image of God that dominates Scripture. The Bible as a whole portrays a God who is more like Hosea (in the book Hosea), pledging to win back the love of his unfaithful bride. Or like the father in Jesus' parable of the lost (prodigal) son who brushes aside his wayward son's apologies and rushes to welcome him back with a feast (Lk 15:20–24).

The image of a vengeful God may come more from our human experience than from our contemplation of the Bible. Why do we find it hard to believe in the father of the prodigal son? Maybe it comes from our own difficulty with whole-heartedly loving and forgiving. And quite possibly many of us have never felt truly loved or totally forgiven in our family relationships. This is where the symbols of "father" and "king" may mislead us. If our experience has led us to believe that fathers and kings are demanding and unforgiving, then we may be led to believe that God is like that, too.

But if we believe that the God who is Love does not want retribution, if we reject the image of a vengeful God demanding that someone pay a blood debt, then why did Jesus have to die? Or did he have to die? And if it was not payment of a debt, then what did his dying achieve?

Because we see Jesus as a special case, we too quickly separate him from the rest of humanity. However, it is precisely in his humanity that we can relate to Jesus. Jesus saves us through his humanity. To find the universal human factors in the death of Jesus, it is helpful to first consider the examples of martyrs, whose humanity is not questioned by anyone.

There are martyrs for the faith who are canonized (officially recognized as saints) by the Catholic church. There are also many other people who have earned common recognition as martyrs or heroes.

Why do we honor and respect these people? To use a well-known example, the Reverend Martin Luther King, Jr. would be a commonly recognized "martyr for a cause." Why do we respect him? We honor Dr. Martin Luther King because he pursued a worthy cause even in the face of clear personal risk. King did not know someone would shoot him that particular day, but he did know that his outspoken defense of equal rights was making enemies, and that some people wished him dead, if that is what it would take to silence him. He could have died of old age if he had stopped speaking, gone home to pastor some small church, and stayed out of politics. But that would have meant giving up on his dream of a nation at peace racially. He would have gone on living physically, but if he felt that he was betraying his mission, he would have felt dead spiritually. He chose to keep on speaking in spite of the personal risk, because he believed that working for civil rights was a mission, the will of God. We honor him because he was faithful to that mission and unselfishly lived for the good of others. He did not allow the fear of death or personal suffering to keep him from pursuing his mission.

We do not honor martyrs because they died; everyone does that, though most people prefer not to think about it, and try to postpone it as long as possible. We do not even respect martyrs because they acted fearlessly or because they died young. Many a criminal has fearlessly faced a violent death and died young, and we judge them foolish and misguided. We honor martyrs and heroes because they lived well, not because they died. They lived according to their beliefs. They lived for the good of others. It is very important to say that martyrs do not choose death. They choose to live with integrity. They choose to be true to themselves and do what they believe to be right. They decide that some things are more important than merely existing for as many years as possible. We might say they choose to live meaningful lives, rather than choosing to merely preserve their existence for a while longer. They live for others, not only for themselves—though they also serve their own deepest need to be true to themselves. If they compromised their sense of mission, they would compromise their own identity. The psychiatrist M. Scott Peck, in his popular book *The Road Less Traveled*, identifies this self-fulfilling service to others as a fundamental component of mental health, which he equates with spiritual health. It is the key idea in the Prayer of St. Francis, which compares many forms of giving to dying to self. In a less absolute form, it is the popular wisdom "in giving, we receive." And it is that quote from Jesus, "For whoever wishes to save his life will lose it, but whoever loses his life for my sake and that of the gospel will save it" (Mk 8:35). In other words, there is a universal human wisdom here; that human beings find themselves by living for others, not in a slavish way of being controlled but by the free choice to do what is good and beneficial for all.

What of Jesus? While biblical quotes are not necessarily the exact words of Jesus, most scholars would agree that Jesus had a clear sense that he was called to a mission. "Did you not know that I must be in my Father's house?" (Lk 2:49). He was to fulfill the expectation of salvation found in the Jewish Scriptures (Lk 4:14–21). It is worth noting that the Scripture passage Jesus reads proclaims that he has come "to bring glad tidings to the poor...liberty to captives and recovery of sight to the blind, to let the oppressed go free" (Lk 4:18–19). There is nothing in the passage about dying. It is all life-giving: healing, freeing, bringing life in its fullness. This focus on life would summarize the mission of Jesus: "I came so that they might have life and have it more abundantly" (Jn 10:10).

However, Jesus met with a lot of resistance, particularly from the establishment, the religious leaders of the Jewish people. In the gospels, we see that Jesus eventually decided that he must confront the religious leaders, but that was asking for trouble. Many of the religious leaders saw Jesus as a threat, probably for a variety of reasons. Some of the Jewish leaders may have rejected him because he challenged their personal comfort and importance. Some Pharisees, like Saul of Tarsus later on, may have opposed Jesus because they did not approve of his interpretation of Scripture. Probably many of his opponents had more pragmatic motivations. At that time, the religious leaders not only had religious authority, they also had a lot of civil governing authority, though they were under Roman overlords. They apparently feared that Jesus would stir up political unrest and bring the wrath of the Roman army down on Israel, which had maintained some local autonomy as a minor province in the Roman Empire. (This was a well-founded fear. About forty years later, in 70 AD, the Roman army did crack down, destroying the Jewish temple and ending any local Jewish power.) The Jewish leaders who worried about this threat thought it politically expedient to suppress Jesus.

Whatever the reasons for their antagonism, Jesus knew it would be dangerous for him to confront the leaders, but he decided he had to do it as a necessary part of bringing God's word to the whole Jewish people. In the Gospel according to Mark 8:31–33, Jesus announces that he must go to Jerusalem, (where the temple is, the center of Jewish worship), and that he will suffer and die there. Peter gives the usual human response; he basically says, "If it is dangerous, don't go!" With the words "Get behind me, Satan," Jesus is saying in essence, "Don't tempt me!" (Don't tempt me to run away from my mission.) We don't have any exact dialogue here, but it is obvious that at some point Jesus realized that pushing his religious message (challenging hypocrisy? preaching liberation from fear of the religious law?) would get him in trouble with the religious leaders, and they would try to stop him. Did he know that he would die? Scripture scholars generally do not think we can verify from Scripture exactly what Jesus knew, but it is logical to assume that Jesus, like Dr. Martin Luther King, could "read the handwriting on the wall." As an intelligent person, he would realize that if he persisted, they might eventually kill him. Naturally, he was tempted to run away from danger, just as we all would be. His close friend Peter didn't want Jesus risking death, either. Peter wanted Jesus to save himself by avoiding confrontation. The same temptation is seen in a more stylized form in Mt 4:3–4, where Jesus is tempted by the devil to turn stones into bread, i.e., to look out for his own comfort.

So Jesus knew that he faced the risk of death. This is the challenge that any martyr faces; they must decide how persistent they will be in the face of danger. Martyrs are those who accept that risk because they choose to live their mission. They choose to be faithful to themselves, their God, their beliefs. Jesus did not let the natural fear of suffering and death keep him from being who he was. He did not let the fear of death conquer him. He was afraid; his words in the garden, "Father, if you are willing, take this cup away from me" (Lk 22:42), show that he dreaded suffering, as anyone would. But he did not let fear stop him; he finishes by saying "not my will but yours be done." Death itself did not destroy him as a person. The resurrection attests to Jesus' victory over death. He maintained his personhood, his integrity, in spite of death.

Did Jesus have to die? It might be truer to say that he had to live. (As we all must!) Ultimately, faithfulness required that he accept death as the price he would pay for his mission, so in that sense, yes, he had to die. But he did not die because God demanded suffering. He died because a sinful world fought the truth he preached, and he had to be true to himself and his mission in life. However, in accepting death, he made a "final statement" that living in faith is the way to wholeness and life. He showed that death need not defeat us. In Mark 15:34, Jesus' final prayer from the cross, "My God, my God, why have you forsaken me?" is the first line of Psalm 22, a psalm which expresses confidence that God will save the faithful person in spite of great suffering. (It does not promise that God will save us from suffering!)

As Christians, we proclaim that Jesus freed us from death. But we know that we will still die, so what does that proclamation mean? It might be more true to say that Jesus offers us freedom from the fear of death, or better yet, freedom from being compromised by the fear of death. He gave us the example of his own life, a human life well lived. He did not compromise his values or beliefs out of fear. This is a liberating message. We have a perfectly natural fear of death because earthly life is the only life we know. But the revelation of Jesus' life, death, and resurrection is that there is more to human life than this mortal existence, which we know will end someday no matter what we do. Jesus reveals that our personhood, our soul or spirit, lives in spite of death. And that by choosing life, choosing to affirm and live what is life-giving, we will live in wholeness in union with God, who is Life.

Discussion Questions:

• How has my understanding of God changed over the years? Do I fear a vengeful and punishing God? Do I see God as One who always loves me and offers me a fuller life?

• What does the death of Jesus have to do with me?

• How am I liberated by the life, death, and resurrection of Jesus?

• Most of us are not threatened with actual death for following our beliefs, but we may be threatened with smaller losses. Have I ever felt the threat of loss if I was to follow God's will?

CHAPTER NINE

Sacraments

Contents
This chapter will explain basic Christian beliefs about the sacraments, organized under some of the key words and concepts in Catholic teaching. The last section of the chapter very briefly describes the seven official sacraments celebrated by the Catholic Church, with longer notes on some of the issues causing particular confusion or conflict among Catholics today. (A more complete exploration of the sacraments, looking more closely at the various symbols and rituals, their meanings and effects, would quickly become a book of its own, so I have consciously limited this chapter.)

The celebration of the sacraments has always been central to Christian worship and beliefs. The sacraments are concrete enactments of our core beliefs about our relationship with God and of who we are as Christians and as church. But people have a great many questions about the sacraments and what we are supposed to believe. What do sacraments do? Do bread and wine really become the body and blood of Christ? Is that a magical belief? Are sacraments really only symbols? Is it truly necessary to be baptized in order to be saved? What do we mean by saying sacraments give grace?

Sign, Symbol, and Sacrament
Let us start with the word "sign," because that was the word generally used to describe the sacraments until 30 or 35 years ago. The widely used Baltimore Catechism defined a sacrament as "an outward sign instituted by Christ to

give grace"(Question 304). More recently, many grade school youngsters have been learning a definition that sacraments are "outward signs of inner grace." For a long time, I taught the definition that "sacraments are sacred symbols of what God is doing in our lives." The key idea in all of these is the same: sacraments are signs/symbols celebrating and bringing about an encounter with God.

It is important to emphasize that dual characteristic; sacraments both celebrate something that is happening and they cause what they celebrate. Sacraments celebrate our belief in God's presence and healing power. At the same time, they enable us to experience God's touch and be made whole.

In the last thirty years, scholars have insisted that we distinguish between simple signs or signals, which convey a single specific message, and symbolic signs, which are much more complex. Simple signs would be things like stop signs or traffic lights, which have one specific meaning given to them and must be learned because the meaning would not be recognized naturally. In contrast, sacraments are symbolic signs or symbols which have natural meanings. Symbols are multidimensional and potentially powerful. They speak to the emotions as well as the mind. Symbolic meanings tend to arise from the nature of the symbol itself, and generally there are numerous meanings possible. For example, water can be lifegiving, cleansing, and refreshing, or changeable, chaotic, and threatening. All of those meanings are symbolized in the water of baptism: we are lost in the flood, the chaos of a sinful world, but we are then raised from it, saved, and cleansed, as the world was cleansed by the flood in the story of Noah's ark. Sleep can symbolize rest or ignorance; the apostles were "asleep" in the garden at Gethsemane, showing they did not understand what was happening. Darkness symbolizes confusion, fear, danger, or evil. Light symbolizes knowledge, truth, or good. Jesus is called the Light of the world, leading us out of that confusion and evil. We use the large Easter candle to represent the guiding presence of the risen Christ in our lives.

The sacraments are powerful symbols, mediating between our material world and invisible spiritual realities. Actually, sacraments are rituals (symbolic actions) with several important symbols and with profound meanings that we can return to again and again to find another level of understanding each time. This is another characteristic of symbols: they are rich in meaning, and we can discover more of that meaning each time we return to celebrate the same symbol or ritual. The Eucharist, especially, we celebrate over and over, so that we might more fully be joined to Christ, whose presence nourishes and sustains us spiritually just as bread nourishes the body.

Symbol and Reality

People sometimes ask if the sacraments, particularly the Eucharist, are symbolic or real. But the definition of symbol is "tangible reality re-presenting or making visible, intangible reality." The tangible material reality (something physical, such as bread, which can be seen, touched, tasted, heard, or smelled) is a vehicle communicating the spiritual reality, which we otherwise cannot see. Both are real. Even with non-religious symbolism, it is obvious that important symbols are taken seriously. A wedding ring is not just another piece of jewelry. A nation's flag is not just a piece of cloth to patch the seat of one's jeans. Symbols have become more than just objects; in a real sense, they are what they symbolize. And because they are what they symbolize, they are powerful and must be respected. That is why I used to tell my students that they could never put the word "only" in front of the word "symbol." To do so is a failure to take symbol seriously; a failure to recognize the power of symbols to make spiritual reality present to us. If symbols were only objects, it would be perfectly all right to use the flag for a doormat, or trade your wedding ring for a new video game, but we know instantly that such behavior would be profoundly offensive. We know that these objects are more than just objects. They stand for, or stand in for, a larger reality. Disrespect for the flag or a wedding ring is seen as disrespect for the nation or the marriage. People are outraged at flag burning. People take wedding rings seriously, too, though the ring is a secondary symbol of marriage, not the most important one. The most important and very natural symbol of marriage is the symbolic act of lovemaking, a physical expression of a deep personal relationship. Again, we know it is very hurtful when that is not respected. Real symbol is serious stuff, because it is powerful. It gives concrete reality to what is otherwise hard to grasp.

In the Eucharist, we celebrate the real presence of Jesus made visible, able to be touched and tasted. According to the words of our traditional teaching, Christ is present "through the appearance of bread and wine." What we see appears to be bread and wine; it tastes, smells, feels, and looks like bread and wine. A chemical analysis would identify it as bread and wine. In other words, the chemical, material, physical reality is bread and wine; that is not what changes. But the physical reality ceases to be the important reality. The physical reality has become a vehicle, making present for us another, equally real and far more important invisible reality: the reality of Jesus, who is as essential to our spiritual life as bread is to physical life. (In our overly bountiful modern culture, we might miss this, but through most of history bread was the "staff of life." If you didn't have bread, you didn't have anything and had little hope of living.) But returning to our question of what is real: in our sacramental celebration, the material reality is not changed, but the essential, most significant reality is changed. In other words, the reality that is really important (the substance) has changed. This is what is meant by the traditional teaching that the bread truly becomes the body of Christ and the wine becomes the blood of Christ (transubstantiation). It is a faith statement about meaning, not a chemistry statement about physical matter.

The wine communicates another core belief: that Jesus lived and died to give us life, just as the grapes were given, sacrificed, to produce wine. However, this symbol also tells us that the gift of Jesus' whole life—his sacrifice and especially his blood poured out on the cross—produced life not death, just as wine produces a life-filled sensation. (In most cultures, blood is a symbol of life, not death. Many religions offer blood to the gods as worshipful acknowledgement of the source of life. Animals were sacrificed at the Jewish temple, and the blood was poured on the altar.)

In the Eucharist, we truly are touched by and nourished by the real Jesus through these symbols of bread and wine. So the sacraments are symbol and reality; the physical symbol enables us to encounter the otherwise intangible spiritual realities. But sacraments are not magic. The words and ritual do not automatically have a spiritual effect. They present an opportunity to encounter God, but we must enter into the ritual with faith to experience the nourishing, healing presence of God.

This renewed awareness that the power of the sacraments is mediated through the rituals has prompted the church to be more conscientious about celebrating them well. For example, we may be more aware that Christ nourishes us if we use bread that looks and tastes like bread. We may be more aware that being a Christian is a dying to an old life of sin and confusion and rising to a new life guided by the light of Christ, if the baptismal ritual involves "burial" in the waters of a tomb-like baptistry and ascending steps on the other side to be handed a lighted candle and a fresh garment. Believable symbols speak to us more forcefully!

Are Sacraments Necessary for Salvation?

Do we need the sacraments to be saved? Yes, because we human beings are physical creatures who tend to trust what we can see. We need to celebrate our faith in concrete ways. Praying and enacting our faith in community with other believers nourishes our faith and helps us truly recognize God reaching out to us. Going through the rituals and giving our responses helps us enter more fully into the experience that is celebrated. The ritual of the sacrament helps us respond to God. Doing is more real than just thinking. This means we need the sacraments, and we need to celebrate them well. But no, the sacraments are not absolutely necessary. Even the church does not have a monopoly on God; God is not under our control like some kind of genie to be let out at our command. God does not have to wait for the official church to act.

St. Peter learned that lesson when he discovered that the Holy Spirit had descended on gentiles who had not yet been baptized. The church, still an all-Jewish community, was not yet convinced that non-Jews could be real Christians. (Jesus was, after all, the Jewish Messiah!) The Holy Spirit had to act first. When Peter saw evidence of the Spirit's presence in these people, he realized that God had chosen to accept gentiles. He knew then that if the church was to be Christ's visible presence in the world, it had to celebrate God's action. That meant the church had to accept these people into the church through baptism (Acts 10:44–49).

In later years, the church did teach that baptism was necessary for salvation, but then qualified that teaching with concepts such as "baptism of blood" and "baptism of desire," recognizing that God could reach people other ways, even if the sacraments are the ordinary way we most powerfully experience God's touch. (See chapter 1, Faith, for an explanation of these concepts.)

Grace

What do we mean by saying sacraments give grace? What exactly is grace? For starters it is not something, it is someone. It is being graced, freely blessed, with the presence of God. When we pray "Hail, Mary, full of grace," we are greeting Mary, who was fully open to the power of God entering into her life. The sacraments help us be open to the life of God, so that we too can be graced with the presence of God. Our faith teaches us that God is always and everywhere present. God is always reaching out to us, like the father in the story of the "prodigal son" who watched for his lost son to return. But we do not always see God waiting or hear God knocking. Celebrating the sacraments helps us hear, see, and feel the presence of the unseen God. God does not need the sacraments, but we often do.

Why do we sometimes feel as though we receive nothing from the sacraments? That is because they are not magic; they do not "work automatically." We have to be "tuned in" to God's presence, which is exactly what the sacraments are supposed to help us do. Consider this comparison: God is always present, just as there are always radio waves around us, carrying many kinds of music. But we cannot hear the music until we have the right radio equipment, and we will still not hear it until we tune in. Or consider that the sun shines every day, but it may not light our life if we don't open the curtains, or if clouds shadow our world so that we cannot see. Distractions, doubts, or the poor example of others who call themselves believers may cloud a person's vision of God. We need to work at staying tuned in and open to God's presence. We will be graced with the presence of God to whatever extent we are open to God. Frequent celebration of the sacraments helps us believe. It helps us be open to the presence of God, but only if we enter into the celebration prayerfully and attentively. And again, God is not limited to our formal church celebrations. Some people may encounter God very powerfully in other ways, too. Nature, the awe-inspiring handiwork of God, has always been a powerful symbol enabling many people to see God. That sense of awe is heard in the popular use of the word "miracle"—the "miracle" of a baby's birth, the "miracle" of creation. And sometimes other people, through their love and loyalty, are "Christ-bearers" to us, which is what the name "Christopher" means. Christians are reminded to be Christ to others. The Hebrew creation stories say essentially the same thing. In Genesis we are told that there is something fundamental about human nature that is meant to image or reflect God.

Seven Sacraments

After many centuries, the church settled on seven official sacraments. (Christian tradition has continued the biblical symbolism of the number seven, which means complete. Many of our traditionally memorized lists have seven items; for example, the seven gifts of the Holy Spirit, the seven spiritual works of mercy, and so on.) The Catholic church continues to celebrate seven sacraments, though many of the Protestant churches have dropped some of them, and often do not give sacramental celebration as central a place in worship. The seven official sacraments celebrate specific religious experiences, but in a sense they also celebrate God's presence and redeeming power in all the important moments of our lives.

Over the last generation, the way we understand and celebrate the sacraments in the Catholic church has changed, in some cases considerably. In fact, all of the sacraments have undergone considerable changes a number of times through the centuries. The goal is always to clarify and more faithfully communicate the unchanging reality of God's saving gift of life. The form or the way we celebrate may change, but the reality of God's gracious gift of life does not change. God does not change; however, our understanding of what God offers does grow, which is why we need to continue studying our beliefs. There are many books available on the sacraments, so this chapter will just give a brief overview.

Each of the seven sacraments celebrates a particular element in our faith. The first three, baptism, confirmation, and Eucharist, together called the sacraments of initiation, celebrate what it means to be a Christian. Two other sacraments, reconciliation and anointing, celebrate healing and reunion with Christ and the church community. And the last two, matrimony and holy orders, celebrate two particular ways of life through which people may be called to represent Christ to others.

Baptism, Confirmation, and Eucharist: Celebrating Christian Identity

Baptism celebrates turning away from the darkness and confusion of sin, which would overwhelm and destroy us like the great flood, and turning to a new life with Christ as our guiding light. When well celebrated, the symbols walk us through an experience of being saved from chaos and drawn forth to a new life guided by Christ in his community, the church. And because we come to know and be saved by Christ through the witness of the church community, our baptism is also our entrance into that saving church community. We become part of Christ and part of the Christian community which brings us to Christ.

Confirmation celebrates "the other side of the coin." We cannot really separate baptism from confirmation, any more than we can separate the two sides of one coin. We may only look at one side, but the other is there, even if hidden. If we enter into the body of the Christ community, the church, then we also inherit the mission of the church. As we become part of that saving body of Christ community, which is filled with the power of the Holy Spirit, we are called to witness to others. Baptism, especially for children, focuses on the entrance into the community. Confirmation focuses on the other side of the coin, mission. Through the laying on of hands and anointing with oil we are reminded that as Christians we share in Christ's mission as priest, prophet, and king. We share in Christ's priestly mission to bring God and humankind together in worship, Christ's prophetic mission to proclaim God's truth, and Christ's kingly mission to establish God's good order in the world. These three tasks are not an option added later; they are implied in baptism. In simple form, that anointing ritual is included in the baptism ceremony for infants, even when a separate confirmation is planned years later.

Our initiation into the church is completed by the Eucharist, the central and constantly repeated celebration of Christian identity. We are the community centered in Christ who nourishes and sustains us. We are the community called to carry on the work of Christ through the ages. Christianity is not a private faith, as some religions are. We are most concretely being "church" when we gather in community to celebrate, be nourished by, and witness to the saving presence of Christ in our midst. My parish put together the statement, "In Christ, we are bread for one another: broken... We gather. Nourished... We reach out."

Why is it that we commonly separate these three sacraments, and usually celebrate them out of their logical sequence? Our present situation resulted from a series of historical events.

In the early church, new Christians were usually adults, though they might bring whole families, children, and even servants, with them. They went through a long preparation period, sometimes years, of learning to live as Christians. When judged ready, they were initiated into the church with baptism, confirmation, and their first Eucharist at the Easter vigil, very consciously celebrating a new life joined to the death and resurrection of Jesus.

Centuries later, the church in Europe lived in a very different world. Nearly everyone was a baptized Christian, except for young children. In the European church (the Roman Rite) it became customary to separate the three initiation sacraments with children (who were generally the only ones being baptized), and exact practices varied over the years. Because of a too-literal concern that baptism was necessary for salvation, people were in a hurry to get infants baptized, so it became customary to baptize very soon after birth. However, a bishop, the official head of the church who traditionally confirmed new members, might not be available for long periods of time, so the rest of initiation was postponed. (It is interesting to note that Eastern Rite Catholic churches take a different approach. They allow the priest to be the ordinary minister of confirmation, and celebrate all three initiation sacraments with infants.) Centuries later in our Roman Rite, it was decided that children who had been baptized as infants were growing in their moral life, and needed the nourishment of the Eucharist and the opportunity to seek God's forgiveness in confession, so these two sacraments began to be celebrated by still-unconfirmed children. This was part of a larger shift in focus away from communal identity toward individual spiritual needs, a characteristic of western culture in general. (One of the goals of recent liturgical reform in the Catholic church has been to reclaim our sense of community in the way we celebrate the sacraments.) Through the centuries, then, the traditional order of the sacraments was abandoned, and the theoretical unity of the three initiation sacraments disrupted.

Finally, in our last generation or so, there has been much concern that in our pluralistic and individualistic culture, young people in their teens need a meaningful celebration of the faith that was handed to them in infancy, to keep them from drifting away from the church. So now confirmation in this country is not usually celebrated in early grade school as it was in the 1950's, but is more commonly postponed until at least the early teens. There is still much disagreement on the best age. Some people who see the sacrament as the celebration of one's Christian commitment, argue that it is not psychologically appropriate to ask young teens to make such a commitment. Those people would prefer that confirmation be celebrated in the late teens or adulthood, when it could be a genuine celebration of personal commitment. Others argue that the sacrament was never meant to be an individual's coming of age ritual, and that we should focus on the support God offers us through the church, a support that young people need as they enter the teens. These people generally prefer to celebrate confirmation at grade school age, in the hope that it will strengthen the young person's identity with the church before they face the challenges of the teen years.

Others argue for liturgical consistency: celebrating the initiation sacraments in the proper order, if not all at the same time. This would mean confirming children before they receive First Eucharist; logically, all three of the initiation sacraments come before the sacrament of reconciliation. One relevant practice is that children of school age who are being received into the church often go through a catechumenate program, at their level of course. They then celebrate all the initiation sacraments at Easter, just as adults in the R.C.I.A. (Rite of Christian Initiation of Adults) now do. This does not address the question of infants and children raised in the church, though.

One thing is certain: we must make every effort to prepare candidates for any sacrament with sensitivity to their age. It is not developmentally appropriate to tell 13-year-olds that they are making an adult commitment. We do not treat them as adults in any other way. In fact, it is developmentally appropriate for them to be suspending commitment for several years while they question everything they have ever been told! We can emphasize community, belonging, and becoming a responsible member of the community, with the understanding that they are only in the process of discovering their place in the church. And we must be careful to respect their wishes if they decide they do not want to celebrate the sacrament. It is fraudulent to present the sacrament as a personal decision, and then pressure them into going through the motions to please others!

Meanwhile, it has become standard practice to follow the R.C.I.A. with adults being received into full communion with the Catholic church. If they were never baptized, they will receive all three initiation sacraments at the Easter vigil. If they are baptized Christians, they will complete the sacraments they have missed. It is hoped that this renewal of the early church practice will help all believers see the links between these three sacraments, and their powerful message about who we are as Christians.

Reconciliation and Healing

Two sacraments celebrate the healing and reconciliation that was so obvious in the ministry of Jesus. These reaffirm God's love for us, and our bond with God's healing, saving community, the church.

The sacrament of reconciliation, also known as penance or confession, celebrates God's forgiveness and our reunion with God and community. It is more than that. It is reconciliation with God, others, and all of God's creation, for sinfulness is inherently self-centered and destructive, alienating us from God, from others, from our proper relationship with the rest of the world, and even from an honest knowledge of ourselves. We have been fractured, broken, by sin, and need healing.

Our understanding and practice of this sacrament has changed a great deal since the liturgical reforms after Vatican II, the council in the early 1960's. Many of us grew up with the word "confession," which focused on the act of telling our sins. For a while we used the word "penance," with its emphasis on an attitude of sorrow and the effort to reform and make up for our sins. Now we use the word reconciliation, drawing our attention to the result we seek, the healing of broken relationships with God and others. The church has also been trying to reclaim the communal element to this sacrament. All sacraments should include the church community. None of them are meant to be strictly private. Private confession was actually a very late development in history.

For centuries, the only celebration of this sacrament was a very public reconciliation for publicly known sinners who had caused scandal to the whole church. Private confession grew out of a completely separate monastic custom of having regular meetings with a spiritual director or friend in the faith, who would help the individual reflect on his or her journey toward God. In time, this pious practice spread beyond the monasteries, and it became common for ordinary believers who wished to grow in their spiritual lives to seek a spiritual director. This practice eventually replaced the little-used public reconciliation, which did not address the needs of the average person, since the sins of most people do not cause a public scandal. Once this private practice was officially recognized as a sacrament, it was decreed that confession must be made to a priest, not just any Christian, with the presumption, no doubt, that a priest would be a more reliable spiritual guide.

As a church community we are again trying to rediscover meaningful ways to celebrate this sacrament. Individual private confession is still the norm, but communal reconciliation services have become familiar, providing an opportunity to pray together, recognizing our common need to confront our sinfulness and turn to God and each other for reconciliation, the healing of relationships which have been damaged. Communal services are normally followed by the opportunity for private confession, since according to current Catholic church law, individual confession to a priest is considered necessary for a full celebration of the sacrament (barring unusual circumstances). But many otherwise active Catholics are not celebrating this sacrament. It seems obvious that as a faith community we are not really comfortable with our current celebration of it. We need to continue to reflect, to pray, and to grow in faith, as we search for meaningful ways to celebrate our joyful recommitment to the journey from darkness to light begun at baptism. God's forgiveness has not changed and will not change. But our celebration of it has changed and will change again.

The anointing of the sick (which for years was called Extreme Unction or the Last Rites) is another sacrament that has changed significantly. For centuries, most people considered it a preparation for death. Now it is recommended for all those suffering an illness that is serious enough to be a burden. Illness often causes anger, fear, and doubt, alienating us from God and other people. The sacrament celebrates our confidence in God's healing presence, which always offers a healing of the spirit, and may also bring about physical healing. This recalls the many healing miracles in the gospels, in which the bodily healing is a sign that Jesus heals the spirit. Again, this sacrament is supposed to include the sacramental church community, who are the vehicle bringing that healing presence of God to their sick members. Like the other sacraments, our celebration of God's healing presence in and through the community has suffered from our limited, overly individualistic focus. We are now trying to reclaim the communal dimension by encouraging celebration with the larger community as much as possible. Some churches have communal services for those who can come to the church building, or celebrate the sacrament in the context of the Sunday Mass, as ways to overcome the alienation and separation that illness may cause.

Matrimony and Holy Orders: Called to a Way of Life

Matrimony and holy orders are sacraments celebrating two particular vocations, two of the particular ways in which people are called to live out our common Christian vocation to be Christ to others. All Christians are called to lives of dedication to God's work. These two vocations are formally celebrated as sacraments. Not that these two vocations are holier than others! Any life lived in Christ is holy. Nuns or brothers who take vows in religious orders, for example, are clearly called to witness to Christ, but there is no formal sacrament to celebrate that life choice.

Matrimony celebrates the life-giving gift of faithful love lived out between a couple, mirroring the life-giving love of God for humankind. All people are called to love others, of course, but this sacrament recognizes that the married couple is called to embody this in a very visible and unique way. Their day-to-day relationship is the sacrament, the sacred symbol of God's kind of love. We find this beautiful theology expressed in the Bible. Unfortunately, the pagan Greek discomfort with the body and sex has often seriously marred teachings on marriage. Since Vatican II, the church has been working to develop a more complete appreciation of this relationship.

Our current disagreements concerning this sacrament are not about the form of the celebration, but about marriages that fail. The Roman Catholic Church teaches that a valid marriage cannot be dissolved. (It is worth noting, though, that this again reflects the more legally focused character of the western church. The Eastern Rite churches have taken a different approach. While teaching that marriage is supposed to be permanent, their tradition accepts that this may sometimes be too great an expectation in our sinful world. Divorce and remarriage are allowed, but the second marriage is not recognized as a sacramental sign of God's kind of love, since the symbol of permanence has been compromised.)

In our Roman Rite, failed marriages can sometimes be annulled. Annulment is the church's decision that a particular couple never did enter into a marriage valid according to church law. Church law involves much more than civil law. (The marriage was, of course, valid under civil law. A couple must get a civil divorce before seeking annulment. And to address one frequent concern: The legitimacy of the children is a civil issue related to inheritance and other legal rights. Their legitimacy is in no way affected by annulment.) Because so much incorrect information is still circulating, particularly in the popular press, let us repeat: Church law does not consider Catholics to be in the state of sin because they are divorced. Divorced Catholics may receive communion and serve in parish positions just as any other members of the community. However, if they want to remarry in the Catholic church, they must first obtain an annulment of the former marriage. Many people who have gone through the annulment process have found it to be an important part of their healing. Essentially, it is a discernment process that seeks to understand why the marriage failed. (I would suggest that this is most helpful when one is at the proper stage in the healing process. It is a rude jolt to have to come back to it years later when planning a second marriage.) Unfortunately, it is structured as a court process, concluding with a ruling on the marriage. This can seem very threatening, particularly to Catholics who fear that the church will judge them harshly. To allay some of that fear, we might note that most annulments sought are granted. In other words, in most cases the official church recognizes that something fundamental truly was missing from the first marriage from the beginning, though often both parties had the best of intentions.

In the past century, the reality of marriage in our culture has undergone great change. The church's theological understanding of marriage has grown, too, with a greater appreciation of the psychological elements of the relationship rather than just the legal form. In past centuries the church granted very few annulments, and these were usually based on the legal procedure itself, or on some clear legal reason why the marriage never should have been allowed according to church law. Examples would be a close blood relationship such as brother and sister, serious mental impairment, or impotence at the time of marriage. Today annulments are far more common; most often they are based on a judgment that either one or both partners did not understand, did not really intend, or were not psychologically capable of making the promises they made, due to psychological impediments, immaturity, or dishonesty. Immaturity here is not simply a question of a person's legal age but may reflect a deeper understanding of psychological maturity. Psychological impediments sometimes refer to addictions or other serious problems, but often the problem involves being brought up in a troubled family, an experience which did not prepare the young adult psychologically for entering a healthy, intimate relationship. Divorced Catholics today, even if they were married for twenty years and had six children, should not assume that a request for annulment is unreasonable. They may have tried very hard to make a relationship work, only to eventually conclude that it was seriously flawed from the start.

The church clearly needs to work on preparing young couples better for marriage, and on supporting married couples as they seek to grow into their marriage relationship. Unfortunately, that is not entirely a solvable problem. It seems to be part of the common human experience that we do not realize how much guidance we need until we have fallen badly!

Many theologians and people working with the church's annulment process are saying that the church needs to do a thorough restudy of our beliefs about marriage in light of our modern knowledge of human psychology, and come up with a process of dealing with failed marriages that is more healing for all concerned. This is a very complex subject. We expect more of the marriage relationship today, partly because we have a better understanding of psychological needs, but probably also because we no longer see marriage as essentially an economic partnership. In the past many married couples stayed together for economic reasons. The husband couldn't envision living without all the services that were expected from a wife, and she couldn't understand how she could live without his income. Many people stayed together out of a sense of duty, even when the relationship was destructive. Today we have concluded that it is not healthy or virtuous to stay in a relationship that remains destructive despite our best efforts.

There is also a growing awareness that marriage is not something that happens all at once on the wedding day. People in their twenties still have a lot of maturing to do, and some of that maturing is only done in the process of trying to live as a married couple. Some people question whether it is realistic to expect people of any age to know themselves and each other well enough to know if their promises are wise or even possible. Many theologians today see the scripture statements on the permanence of marriage as an ideal, a goal, much the way we interpret "turn the other cheek," another statement from the same sermon on the mount (Mt 5:39). In that same sermon, the teaching about divorce immediately follows the statements telling us to tear out our eye or cut off our hand if they cause us to sin. The church takes all these teachings seriously, but not literally; they are considered dramatic statements calling us to firmly reject sin. Our Christian brethren in other denominations take the same view of the teaching on marriage. They agree with the Catholic church that couples should strive to make marriage a lifelong, loving commitment, but they treat this as an ideal, not as a literal command, any more than chopping off your hand is a command.

The other official sacrament of vocation is holy orders, which celebrates the anointing of a bishop, priest, or deacon in service to the church community. Again, every baptized person has been called through the laying on of hands to share in Christ's priestly work of bringing God and humankind together, but ordained ministers are called in a special way to be visible and official leaders of the priestly community's worship and witness.

Our debates about the sacrament of holy orders rarely have anything to do with the celebration of the sacrament. Most Catholics have never even attended an ordination. However, there is heated dissension over who should be accepted into the priesthood. Until recently women were not accepted as priests or ministers in any of the Christian churches, or for the most part, as public leaders of any kind in our society. In the last generation, many Protestant communities have begun to ordain women to their priesthood or ministry. However, the Catholic church continues to teach firmly that Christ ordained only men, and that, as the representatives of Christ, it is only fitting that priests be male. In recent years many Catholics, including priests, bishops, and theologians, have questioned whether this is really God's will or whether it is a cultural prejudice from which the church needs to be redeemed. After all, they argue, Jesus only chose Jewish men as his disciples—indeed, only had Jewish followers—but the church decided (after considerable dissension: see Acts of the Apostles) that this was not normative. Addressing this debate, the Catholic church has clearly and emphatically restated that it is God's will that only men be ordained, and this will not change. The issue of women in the priesthood is officially considered a closed topic, not open for further discussion.

The issue of married clergy is much simpler. There is no question that the apostles were married, and married men were priests for centuries. (In contrast, while some people think there is evidence from artwork and texts that women were ordained in the early Christian community, the evidence is not clear and not officially accepted.) The rule against a married clergy was imposed at a particular point in history to deal with abuses and to challenge priests to greater dedication to their ministry. A large number of people agree that the rule against married priests could be changed at any time. The debate is whether or not this change would be good for the church and the priesthood.

Discussion Questions:
- When have I felt most nourished by the sacraments? When have I felt touched by God?
- Have there been times I was disappointed by the celebration of the sacraments? What can I do about that?
- Is the Sunday Eucharist a source of renewal and strength to me each week? Why or why not?
- What could I do to improve my celebration of God's sustaining presence, and my membership in the body of Christ?

Suggested Reading:
Joseph Martos, *The Catholic Sacraments* (Wilmington, DE: Michael Glazier, 1983). Introductory but thorough Catholic reflection on the modern understanding of the sacraments. The author considers sacraments from the vantage points of psychology, sociology, history, and theology, followed by reflections on the implications for Christian worship and life.

CHAPTER TEN

Miracles

Contents

This chapter will endeavor to clarify what Christians believe about miracles. First, we look at the question of reconciling a belief in miracles with scientific thinking. A second subtopic makes a careful distinction between the belief in miracles and the belief in magic. In popular culture they are often confused, but they are fundamentally different beliefs. For Christians it is very important to be able to tell them apart, because we recognize miracles as real actions of the God of life, but we reject magic as false and superstitious.

The miracles of Jesus are an important part of all four gospels. It is evident that many people were attracted to Jesus during his ministry because of the healing he did. People today are still fascinated with miracles, both those in the past and those in the present. For example, many people today have had powerful faith experiences focused on the apparitions of Mary at Lourdes or Fatima. But what exactly do we believe about miracles? Do they still occur? Is a belief in miracles compatible with modern scientific knowledge? And how does belief in miracles differ from belief in magic?

There seem to be two basic ways miracles are commonly understood. One view comes from the medieval European distinction between "natural" and "supernatural." This is the understanding of miracles found in official Catholic church teaching. Miracles are understood to be "beyond the natural." In modern terms, this becomes "an occurrence which cannot be explained according to science." The test for miracles becomes "could this event have occurred naturally?" Following this train of thought, if people pray for a healing, and the doctors cannot give any medical explanation for why the person got well, that would be considered evidence in favor of declaring the healing a miracle. This view tends to see a miracle as a divine suspension of the natural order. The sun standing still would be a good example of this; there does not seem to be any meaning to it other than to prove the presence of a Power greater than nature.

This understanding of miracles presumes two separate worlds, the natural and the supernatural. Something is in one realm or the other, not both. Either someone got well naturally or it was a miracle. One serious problem with this view is that as scientific knowledge advances, there is less and less that cannot be explained by science, thus it gets harder and harder to find events recognized as miracles. In essence, this approach tends to rule out miracles. Another problem is that it may leave people feeling that they have to choose between belief in science or belief in God.

We could make an even stronger statement. This concept of God setting aside the natural order to cause the occasional miracle is actually offensive to many modern believers. It offends the sense of awe and respect for God's creation of the universe. It suggests opposition between God and the created world. To suggest that God has wondrously fashioned the natural order and then interferes with it seems contradictory; God would be contradicting the nature of God's own work.

The understanding of miracles from the Jewish tradition in the Bible is quite different. The ancient Jewish people did not ask if an event could have occurred naturally; they did not make a clear distinction between natural and divine. Everything was assumed to be under divine control. If it rained gently on the fields, God was blessing them; if it flooded, God was punishing them for their sinfulness. But a miracle was extraordinary in that the event was experienced as a notable, unexpected occurrence showing God's care and concern for his people. The escape of the Jews from Egypt was seen as miraculous, a wonderful saving act of God, showing God's power and his love for his people. But biblical scholars today believe that the events of the Exodus can be explained in natural terms also. They conclude that the escaping Jewish slaves traveled light and on foot, and fled across a marshy area while the tide was low, followed by the Egyptian soldiers laden with armor, weapons, and chariots. With all that added weight, the Egyptian soldiers got stuck in the mud, then were overwhelmed by the incoming tide. (Not quite as dramatic as the Cecil B. deMille movie.) From a biblical mindset, though, it was an amazing event. Instead of the disaster that might have been expected, it was a wonder-full salvation by God's intervention.

To the mind of people in biblical times, a natural explanation does not in any way detract from the miraculous character of the event, because natural and divine are not seen as contradictory or mutually exclusive. This escape was experienced by the Jews as a saving act of their God who cared for them. It was such a powerful experience that it became a founding memory cementing their sense of identity. More than any other experience, the Exodus made them a people. It identified what it meant to be a Jew; they were the people saved by God. This memory is so important that it has been relived through the ritual of the Passover celebration for three thousand years to keep alive that awareness that "God is our saving God, and we experienced this most clearly in the miraculous journey out of slavery to the promised land." (For Christians, Jesus added a new dimension to that celebration in identifying himself with the bread and wine of Passover, so that we Christians now celebrate that "God is our saving God, and we experience this most clearly in Jesus' gift of his life and death for us.")

From this perspective, an event can be both natural and miraculous. A growing number of Christians are looking at miracles with this understanding, seeing a miracle as a manifestation of God's presence, power, or healing love, which may be seen through the natural, rather than necessarily outside of the natural. It is an open-ended approach, potentially allowing more events to be experienced as miraculous. It is compatible with science, because it does not challenge the scientific explanation or suggest that some events are contrary to science. This understanding is not in any sense less religious. In fact, it may allow for a greater sense of God's presence and involvement in our world.

The biggest problem with this approach is that there are no clear objective criteria for deciding what is a miracle and what isn't. It is easy to accept the biblical miracles, based on our trust in the Bible. But how do we judge a modern event? We want to be able to say that miracles are truly special events, which is what makes them stand out as signs of God's presence. We do not want to suggest that "it's a miracle if you think it is."

Should we be able to define some objective criteria for recognizing an event as a miracle? Requiring objective criteria is essentially a scientific approach. Should we expect to have a scientific way of proving a spiritual reality? Actually, our present definition that a miracle is an event beyond scientific explanation, may only show the limits of our scientific knowledge. We can't say that science will never come up with an explanation, only that it is beyond the science we know right now. In short, it doesn't really prove anything; we still must choose to believe. Could we be comfortable saying that a miracle goes beyond any kind of proof, and depends on eyes of faith? Ultimately, no matter how much evidence we cite, when we believe that an event was the act of God we make an act of faith, and the very word "faith" implies that we have gone beyond the realm of proof. It is not possible to prove that something was a miracle. We cannot even prove the existence of God! For a believer there may be evidence, but for a non-believer no proof is possible. As we know from Scripture, even Jesus did not convince everyone with his healings. Some people witnessed these events without seeing anything miraculous about them.

Actually, most of the time the church does not pass official judgment on purported visions or miracles, leaving them as a matter of personal faith. However, when the church is evaluating a canonization case (the official declaration that a person led a holy life and is believed to be a saint in heaven), miracles attributed to the saintly person's intervention are cited as evidence of the person's holiness. In that case, the church has to make a judgment on the validity of the miracle, and begins with results that are deemed "beyond natural explanation."

Miracle vs. Magic

On some issues, there are no differences of opinion within Catholic and other mainline Christian leadership. The Bible makes it very clear that miracles are not magic. To confuse them puts religion in the realm of superstition. The Christian Scriptures, the New Testament, very clearly say that any attempt to work magic is evil. So we must be clear about the difference.

A belief in magic vs. a belief in miracles

Educated people today would usually say that magic is not real. We generally consider it just a form of entertainment. We know the magician is not really doing the things he appears to do. Even if we cannot figure out how he

A BELIEF IN MIRACLES	A BELIEF IN MAGIC
• Miracle: There is no power in any word, action, or object itself.	• Magic: Words, actions, or objects have power.
• Miracle: Only a person in touch with God knows when God is acting, and can point to it and be the vehicle for God's miracle.	• Magic: Anyone who uses the word/action/object makes the magic happen.
• Miracle: There are no "right words."	• Magic: A "magician" only has power if the right word, action, or object is used.
• Miracle: God's communication to us.	• Magic: There is no explanation for why the power exists.
• Miracle: Always for good—reveals God's presence.	• Magic: The power can be used for good or evil purposes.
• Miracle: A person can only be touched by a miracle if he/she is open to belief.	• Magic: Anyone could be a victim of unfair magic.
• Miracle: A sign to show God's presence and action; the purpose is communication, so that we might understand what God is doing.	• Magic: Manipulative; the purpose is to gain control over other people or events; even over God.

does it, we know the magic tricks are just illusions. But to compare magic and miracle, we must take magic seriously. We have to ask, "What do people believe when they believe in magic?" (And of course, there are still many people in the world who do believe in magic. There are religions, such as Voodoo, which clearly include the belief in magic. Psychologists say all children start with a belief in magic for lack of a better understanding of why things happen. And many adults believe that certain objects have the power to bring luck or a curse.)

We are all familiar with magic beliefs. The essentials are found in any children's magic story. The belief in magic is a belief that certain words, objects, or actions have power in themselves. Anyone who speaks the magic words makes something happen. The person does not even have to realize he is doing it, because the power is in the words or wand, not the person. A person can cause magic to happen by accidentally picking up a magic wand or saying magic words. Many stories revolve around getting possession of the magic object, such as a wand, or getting the book of "spells," or learning the magic words. The magician only has power because he knows the words, or has the magic recipe, or whatever. The power is in the word or object. There is no explanation for why the power exists, or where it came from, and it can be used for good or evil. But the person who has possession of the magic has power over others. He or she can turn people into frogs, or control their fate in any number of ways.

To believe such powers really exist is very frightening. It would be unjust for anyone to take control over other people that way. So the attempt to use magic is evil. (Magic shows are not the same. They are not really attempting to control anyone. We know that the "magic" is all illusion.) A real attempt to work magic, such as sticking pins in a doll with the belief that this action would cause injury to some individual far away, would be denying other people their rightful freedom, as well as causing harm in this case. Even so-called "white magic"—magic with a seemingly good intention, such as causing someone to fall in love with you—is manipulative and unfair. Trying to use magic to control God or make God do something according to our wishes is also evil; it is a foolish, presumptuous attempt to be greater than God. This is what the second commandment is actually about. We are told not to take the name of God "in vain" (uselessly). When Moses received the ten commandments, how were people trying to use the name of God? It has been a common belief, in many cultures and through the centuries, that one could call down a curse on another person, asking God to damn or otherwise punish the person you wished to punish. The second commandment reminds us that not only are such attempts pointless, since we cannot control God, but also that it is sinful to try. This quite logically follows from the first commandment, which pronounces that God is God. (And we are not!)

Sometimes religious superstitions attempt to manipulate God. When we were children, many of us were told that we can't trick or manipulate God into letting us into heaven by wearing the right sacred object, such as a scapular, or by saying the right prayers. God is God and cannot be manipulated. Religious rituals or objects are to help us remember to live with faith in God and follow God's will; they do not have power in themselves, like magic amulets. Will wearing scapulars help us reach heaven? "Yes," if it we wear them as a constant reminder to live as Jesus would want us to live. "No," if we are expecting them to work by themselves like magic amulets.

To cite a currently popular and seemingly harmless custom, belief that burying a statue of St. Joseph—upside down!—will aid in getting a house sold would be a modern example of superstition. It is treating the statue like a magical object. Statues or other religious objects, sometimes collectively called sacramentals—literally "little sacraments"—are visual reminders of our faith. They remind us to pray, to live as the saints did, to put our trust in God. Their power is the power to remind us that God is near, the power to inspire us to be more faithful. If they are used as reminders and inspiration, they help strengthen our faith. If they are seen as magic objects or actions having power in themselves, they destroy true faith because if we trust in magic, we think we are in control and no longer need to trust in God or accept God's will. The whole point of magic is to control events according to our will.

Magic is a human attempt to control events, people, and maybe even God. Miracles and sacraments are both visible expressions of God's action. In the Bible, there is a story of St. Peter severely scolding a man who thought he could buy the power to bring the Holy Spirit down in the sacrament of confirmation. The man assumed that there was something magical in doing the ritual correctly, and that if he just knew the right words and gestures, he would have the same power that Peter had (Acts 8:18–22). He thought the power was in the words and actions. He did not understand that the sacraments are signs of what God is doing; they do not control God. We never make God act. We recognize God's presence in miracles, and we celebrate God's action through sacraments, so that we will be better able to respond and to be made whole by the God who is always waiting for us to be open to that gift of life.

If we look at the miracle stories in the Bible, we can quickly find clear differences between miracles and magic. If Jesus had been a magician, he could have made anything happen whenever he wanted to. However, we read that in Nazareth, Jesus was not able to perform any miracles because of their lack of faith (Mk 6:5). So there was no magic in his words or deeds. He was reaching out to people, but he couldn't force anything. People had to respond with faith to experience the healing touch of God. Miracles do not work automatically, as magic is believed to work. Miracles are signs, and signs are only seen by those who have their eyes open. Many stories tell of Jesus healing blindness or deafness. The healing of physical blindness or deafness symbolizes healing of spiritual blindness also. Modern "faith healing" would generally be seen as another expression of this same miraculous power of God, which is not magic and touches only believers. (Faith healing seems to have gotten a bad name. There are frauds in every business, and the frauds make the evening news, but we should not assume that all faith-healing is fraudulent.) The sacrament of anointing celebrates God's healing power, and may bring about a physical healing as well as a spiritual one. Faith is the key to sacraments and miracles. But it does not have to be a perfect faith; there is that wonderful story in which Jesus asks a man if he has faith, and the man answers "I do believe, help my unbelief!" (Mk 9:24).

Not just anyone can work miracles because it is not a matter of learning magic words; it requires a special person. We know Jesus worked miracles to heal people or give life in various ways. But God works through many people. In the Acts of the Apostles, we read of the apostles and other Christians working miracles. Why are people other than Jesus able to work miracles? Because it is the power of God that heals, and God works through faithful followers who are open to that power. In Acts of the Apostles, we read of a church community that is very conscious that Christ continues his saving presence through his faithful followers the church. People who truly allow God to direct their lives would sense when and why a miracle is possible, so these people would be able to be the vehicles manifesting God's power. That is why miracles would logically be evidence that a person performing them was a saint.

A miracle is a sign of God's saving power and presence. In the Gospel according to John, the author used the Greek word for "sign," rather than the word for "miracle." John did not want us to focus on how marvelous the event was, he wanted to emphasize that these acts pointed to something more important, the fullness of life that Jesus offers. (All the gospel writers saw miracles pointing to spiritual healing, of course, but John chose his words to emphasize that point.)

This "pointing to something more important" is what the miracles are all about. That is why only a holy person can be God's messenger, because only a holy person has a sense of what God wills. It is also why a person has to have faith to be healed by a miracle. Only a person of faith is listening to God's message and can be touched by it. Miracles are about faith; the ability to see beyond the surface to recognize the power of the unseen God working in our lives.

Discussion Questions:

• Have I ever experienced a miracle or faith healing?
• We rarely hear of miracles today. Why? Is God less active than in the first-generation church, seen in the Acts of the Apostles? Are we not as open as those Christians were?
• Do people I know seem to believe in magic?
• Have I ever noticed people treating religious objects as magic?

CHAPTER ELEVEN

Sin

Contents

This chapter will look at three quite different concepts; personal sin, original sin, and social sin. All three are sin, indicating a brokenness or alienation in the relationship with God, others, the created world, and even within ourselves. However, the similarity ends there, so they will be treated separately.

Personal Sin: Action or Attitude?

Usually when we talk about sin, we are talking about personal sin, the evil an individual chooses to do. There are two common ways of understanding personal sin. We can focus on the action done, or we can focus on the intention of the person doing it. When we were children, we focused on the action. We were told about many things that we should not do because those actions were sins. (The catechism also mentioned sinful thoughts and sins of omission, but I think most of us did not dwell on those.) We could, at least theoretically, envision a list of all the actions that would be sinful and should be avoided. We considered ourselves good if we avoided those wrong actions. That thinking is all right for children, but it is fundamentally childish.

Unfortunately, years ago adults were often taught that same sort of morality. It was a morality that left the thinking to someone else, someone supposedly wiser, the church authorities. Often, little distinction was made between the authority of major teachings of the official church (the "magisterium") and the interpretations given by any particular priest or nun. (Anyone dressed in black was assumed to be representing "the church.")

Many Catholic adults had the impression that they were not supposed to think. They were just supposed to obey. Perhaps the advice and lists were good, but they did not challenge adults to be fully responsible for their own morality, and they did not raise moral thinking to that more mature level of the gospel challenge to love one another.

One very obvious example of the focus on wrong actions is the way people dealt with the fast and abstinence laws. To begin with, fasting and abstaining are religious practices meant to enhance the celebration of our faith. Morally speaking they are not on the level of the commandments, but in the past these practices seemed to be just as serious to many Catholics. Secondly, people often felt guilty even when they broke a rule by accident and ate a hot dog for lunch on Friday out of forgetfulness. They were taking the action more seriously than the intent, and considering it serious matter when there was not even any inherent evil involved. People were commonly very legalistic, watching the clock at midnight so as not to break the fast, yet often were not nearly as concerned about the spirit of the law. Going out to dinner and eating lobster on Friday kept the letter of the abstinence law, but it certainly wasn't penitential! Many people were generally treating these church fasting laws like taboos, rules-which-must-not-be-broken-because-something-terrible-will-happen, though why the rules were important was not clear.

Especially since Vatican II, the Catholic church has made many changes with the goal of encouraging people to give more attention to the meaning of religious practices. The official fast and abstinence laws have been greatly reduced. People are encouraged to focus less on keeping minor rules and to think more about what we personally should be doing to become more prayerful and more faithful Christians. In this country, the abstinence rules no longer make sense anyway. Originally, meat was forbidden because it was a luxury item for feasts, and fish was the common everyday food. Today, fish is often more expensive than meat, so that if we are to abstain from luxuries, we need to abstain from fish! On the other hand, abstaining from something we don't like is not penitential either. Obviously, this practice needs some thought! And that is exactly the point; we need to take responsibility for practicing our faith thoughtfully.

Even regarding more serious issues, the past focus on particular wrong acts has sometimes created an unfair burden and caused unwarranted feelings of guilt for many people who were sincerely trying to be faithful Christians in an imperfect world. Many adult Catholics today have been alienated from their church or from church authority because they have felt unfairly condemned by church teachings as they understood them. A good example is the large number of Catholics who have left the church as a result of divorce. In past generations annulment was rare, but today most people who apply have their marriages annulled. However, many do not apply out of fear, embarrassment, ignorance, or just a distaste for the court-style process. (Then again, it is not really entirely fair for people to blame the church, if they themselves can't face their past enough to apply for an annulment.)

Why do we, the church, have such a problem with this issue of sin? Part of the problem is the natural tendency of institutions to become legalistic. There is a constant tension in the church, which is supposed to be more than a worldly institution. The church is guided by the Spirit, who blows where it will, much to Peter's surprise (see the Acts of the Apostles). Part of our current tension is due to a radical change in the way many people view church law. Official church law has assumed that canon law (church law) was a straightforward expression of God's will. This conclusion was based largely on an overly simple belief that, between nature and Scripture, God's will was plainly evident and could be defined once for all time. We are much more conscious today that there are two major limits to this clear evidence. For one, the moral teachings in Scripture reflect the knowledge of people in their own time and culture. (For example, there are Old Testament passages which express the belief that God wanted his people to slaughter women and children in enemy towns.) Also, we have become acutely aware that there is still a great deal we do not understand about nature, even our own nature. Science is constantly making new discoveries about the natural order and raising new moral questions. We might say that morality is based on our nature, but if we do not fully know our nature, then we cannot be sure we fully understand what is moral.

If sin is not a set of easily listed wrong actions, what is it? Since Vatican II, the Catholic church has put greater emphasis on sin as the failure to love. This same conflict of views was seen in the Jewish faith at the time of Jesus. For example, the Pharisees considered it essential to keep a long list of specific laws concerning the Sabbath. However, another Jewish tradition, expressed by a Jewish scholar of the law in Luke 10:25–28, stated that the whole law could be summed up in two great commandments: to love God and to love your neighbor. Jesus affirmed the wisdom of that explanation. Jesus repeatedly challenged his fellow Jews to use common sense and recognize that the religious laws were meant to help us live according to God's will; the laws should not be allowed to enslave us (Lk 6:1–11).

Both Jews and Christians have often become so zealous about the law that the laws themselves have been made a god. In contrast, Christian Scriptures teach that choosing to love, choosing what is lifegiving and healing, like pulling an animal out of a ditch even on the Sabbath, is the basic command of God. The Christian Scriptures actually contain very few statements that label certain actions as sins.

This understanding of sin as the failure to love sounds "wishy-washy" to some people at first, but it is actually far more challenging and demands more of us than simply avoiding any list of wrong actions. A law-centered morality can be self-centered and can lead people to the smug sense that they have kept the law perfectly. Jesus gives an example in the story of the Pharisee who, even in prayer, bragged about his righteousness, noting that he fasted and tithed regularly (Lk 18:9–14). This would be comparable to people a few years back who considered themselves good Catholics because they kept fast and abstinence laws and contributed regularly to the collection. In contrast, a morality based on love will challenge us constantly to love more than we have before. We can never say we have loved enough and have finished that obligation. And by love Jesus means more than a warm feeling or even being friendly. Love is doing what is lifegiving. It means doing what Jesus did: healing, forgiving, welcoming, accepting, guiding, challenging, and witnessing a life of faith, even to the point of accepting persecution and death for that witness. There is nothing easy about it, as Jesus himself shows in his agonized prayer in the garden at Gethsemane.

Seeing sin as the failure to love also shifts the focus from the action to the actor. The old Baltimore Catechism that so many of us studied said that something was seriously sinful if it was seriously wrong, we knew it was seriously wrong, and we freely chose to do it (Question 69). We are now giving greater attention to the second and third conditions of that definition. That may be largely due to our growing understanding of psychology. We have come to realize that a person may know a rule without truly understanding the damage caused by breaking it. When a six-year-old shoots someone, we do not put the child in jail; we provide counseling. (And ask why our society so freely leaves guns around!) We also realize that emotionally disturbed people may have such a twisted perception of reality that they do not really act freely. They may do terrible harm but they are victims of illness and need help not just punishment. (If judged dangerous, they must, of course, be prevented from harming others. This may require confinement, which is to protect both the mentally ill person and the public.)

Today even sincere, committed believers are more inclined to consider it presumptuous to believe that we or any church authority know the mind of God. For example, judging from simple anatomy it seems very clear that God created a man to love and be joined with a woman, leading most people to the conclusion that homosexuality was a rejection of God's good plan laid out so obviously in nature. More recently, with new knowledge of genetics and brain chemistry, we have been faced with substantial physical evidence that some individuals are naturally oriented toward homosexual feelings. That is their nature. In other words, their natural psychological orientation doesn't fit their natural anatomical orientation. Sexual orientation rooted in body chemistry is just as real as is anatomy. This leads people to ask how we can be so sure we know what God expects of a person whose psychological nature is at odds with his or her anatomical nature.

The Catholic church teaches that homosexual acts are intrinsically disordered. However, homosexuals themselves should not be condemned or considered sinners for being homosexual since it is not something they choose. In addition, Scripture and the tradition of the church continue to clearly teach that marriage is a union of one man and one woman. Sexual acts outside of marriage are gravely sinful. Unlike a person's orientation actions are chosen. There is no sin in being oriented toward homosexual feelings, but a person is still responsible for avoiding sinful actions. That means homosexuals must remain celibate, as any single person should.

Many of the topics that have caused a lot of disagreement in recent decades, such as homosexuality and birth control, involve theories of "natural law." Many of the moral rules we have been taught depend on an understanding of what is natural and thus presumed to be God's will. The concept of a natural law indicates a very positive belief that moral reasoning is logical and in touch with reality. This natural order is presumed to make sense, and to be—to some degree—obvious, so that people sincerely pursuing the truth will recognize the wisdom of it. At least, it should theoretically be obvious if we know the facts. But do we? Today we are much more aware that we are constantly discovering or coming to a new understanding of human nature. One of the facts we have discovered is that nature is less orderly than we used to think. There is a lot of variability, flexibility, and ambiguity in nature. The concept of a natural law is not necessarily a problem, but presuming that we know nature can be naïve.

Also, some of the facts of our natural world actually change. For example, modern health and longevity, plus urban rather than farm lifestyles, add new elements to the question of healthy and moral decisions about family planning. In developed countries, the nature of the average couple's relationship has changed dramatically over the last century. In earlier centuries, many babies died, and many women died in childbirth. With modern medicine, women almost always survive childbirth, and almost all children survive to adulthood. If every couple followed the old ideal of accepting all the children that God sent, many couples could produce twelve or more healthy children! But we know this would create many problems for the individual families, their communities, and for the global society. How does this change in the nature of families, life expectancy, and population growth affect our perception of God's will for us?

The church today recognizes that married couples may need to limit the number of children they have but considers only natural methods of family planning to be morally acceptable. The reasoning is that artificial forms of birth control (pills, IUDs, condoms, or such) contradict the expression of life-giving openness that should be expressed in marital love-making. It's as though the couple is simultaneously saying both "yes" and "no" to the complete mutual giving of themselves in love. Another consideration is that most of the forms of artificial birth control are, instead, abortifacients, since they do not prevent conception but prevent the development of the new life already conceived. Unfortunately, many couples say they do not find natural family planning to be natural or helpful to their relationship either, since saying "I love you, but no sex this week" also seems contradictory. In practical terms then, it remains an issue of contention within the church.

Limitations in our knowledge or freedom bring us back again to placing greater weight on the intention of a person not on a list of wrong actions. We can certainly judge actions wrong if they are clearly harmful, but we should be slow to judge others guilty of sin.

In our personal decision-making, instead of asking if an action has been labeled a sin, we might better ask: "Are we choosing what will help us, and all of the people involved, to be better people? Is it healing and forgiving, challenging us to greater honesty, consideration, and growth? Is it the kind of thing we can envision Jesus doing?" (I used to think that last question was trite, but I have realized that it works. It takes us to the "gut level," the affective level. We let our conscience really speak to us, unclouded by our usual rationalizations justifying what we want to do!)

Jesus was always bringing people a fuller life in some way. He was healing, forgiving, teaching, challenging, and sometimes correcting the proud or unrepentant. Sin is rejecting or turning away from what is life-giving— "missing the mark" according to the root meaning. Sin is not only the choice to reject God and others, it is the choice not to be true to ourselves. It is choosing not to live fully and authentically; choosing not to be what we are called to be, the image and likeness of God. It is a darkness or death from which we need to be saved. Any dependence on rules or laws must be evaluated in light of the command to love God, neighbor, and self.

At the same time our faith as well as our desire to act as mature Catholics require that we make informed decisions that are based not only on personal intention but on the teaching of the church, which we believe is guided by the Holy Spirit not only in matters of faith but in matters of morality as well.

Original Sin: A Situation, not a Punishment

What are we saying when we say that a baby is born "in the state of original sin"? Clearly, the baby has not made any choice to reject God or do evil. Nor would it make any sense to think that the God who is Love would in any way blame a baby for sins committed by others in the past. The church teaches us that only the light of divine Revelation clarifies the reality of sin and especially of the sin committed at the origin of humankind.

Original sin is a completely different concept from personal sin, which was discussed in the last section. Personal sin is the sin of one's personal choices. Original sin, on the other hand, does not involve personal wrongdoing or guilt. Original sin might better be described as a situation of being alienated from God, self, and others, a situation in which we inevitably find ourselves as part of the human experience.

I have heard two convincing explanations of this state of alienation. My experience as a parent made me acutely aware of one in particular. We recognize that every child comes into moral consciousness already hurt and misguided by the people before us. Consequently, the child is predisposed to hit back, so to speak; that is, he or she is predisposed to sin. In saying that a child is born with original sin, we do not mean to literally connect it with birth or conception. It refers to coming to consciousness as a human decision-maker, a process which takes years.

One of the most popular and long-standing misconceptions about the Bible is that sex is considered sinful. This is even found in the writings of respected theologians of the past, such as St. Augustine, who thought original sin was passed on through the lust of sexual intercourse. But that negative judgment is really from pagan Greek philosophy, not the Bible. Greek philosophy was considered the highest learning in the Roman Empire, so of course, scholars like St. Augustine were well versed in it. Greek philosophy tended to glorify human reason and distrust the body as too animal-like. In contrast, the Bible clearly says that sex is good. God created us as sexual beings and said it was good (see the Book of Genesis, chapter 1). Core church teaching also says sex is good; marriage, a sexual union, is a sacrament. Nothing is holier than a sacrament. Enough said?

Original sin is about spiritual life. Growing into spiritual awareness is a gradual process, and what we are saying is that by the time a child is old enough to make the choice to sin or not, that child has experienced the effects of sin and been misguided by it. Even the best parents can remember times when, from tiredness or frustration, they yelled at or hit a child inappropriately, or left a baby crying because they did not know what else to do. Playmates or siblings are often unfair, not to mention bad influences from TV, music, and the larger culture in general. Many of us can remember unfair discipline, advice, or guidance from parents or others, sometimes given with the best of intentions. And of course, some people have experienced severe mistreatment from adults who were alcoholic or had emotional problems. All of these negative experiences predispose us to angry, defensive, retaliatory, or selfish choices—in other words, personal sin.

Another, also rather compelling view, explains original sin by simply saying that our human nature, like the rest of creation, is inherently flawed or incomplete, lacking the perfection toward which we are called. As St. Paul affirms, "Just as sin came into the world through one man, and death came through sin...sin was indeed in the world before the law" (Rom 5:12–13). To begin, there is a fundamental experience shared by every child, separation from the mother—birth, weaning, the many stages of greater independence—which psychologically may be experienced as unkind desertion. I am not a psychologist, but I think that a lingering sense of being abandoned or unwanted is at the root of much sin.

Social psychologists postulate that natural factors encourage dishonesty among people. Natural selection rewards cheating. For example, a man who fathers more children is more successful genetically, so nature has rewarded him for cheating on his wife. (Does that really affect anyone's behavior? Are genes that favor cheating being passed on? Are there genes that encourage cheating? We don't have answers to any of that; it's all speculation!)

Original sin, whatever the cause, is a universal human situation, from which we all need to be saved. When we celebrate baptism with the infant who is not yet capable of any personal choice to sin, we are celebrating our faith that the child will be saved from this chaos of sin that floods around us. The child will be saved through the power of the Holy Spirit alive in the faith community, guiding that child toward what is good and lifegiving, away from what is destructive. We are celebrating a lifelong experience of salvation through the support, witness, and guidance of the body of Christ community, not just something that happens at one particular moment to the unconscious child.

Social Sin: Systematic Evil

A third kind of sin we hear about more frequently today is social sin. This also is not about the personal choice to sin. Social sin refers to destructive social structures—laws, policies, commonly accepted customs or widely held attitudes—which unfairly and unnecessarily limit human freedom and dignity.

Some of these social structures are formal and written, others are informal, but everyone in the particular society involved knows that this is the way things work. I recall the old movies in which the stereotypical southern police chief tells the newcomer, "Sonny, that's not the way we do things in this town." Examples of social sin would be a law allowing slavery, an unwritten policy of hiring and underpaying illegal immigrants, a widely accepted custom of sexual harassment, or a commonly accepted attitude that people on welfare are worthless cheats and freeloaders. All of these are social structures that shape what a person can do in that particular society, much as walls and doors shape where you can go in a building.

Social sin also includes laws and policies created with good intentions, but which result in situations that are unfair or destructive. For example, there used to be workplace policies designed to protect women from unsafe or unfair work conditions, but these policies became excuses to deny women work or a fair wage. Another example is that of laws which place most school control under local government, on the theory that local people know best how to meet local needs. But if financing is local, poor areas have little to spend, and the children end up with a deficient school system. They do not have learning opportunities equal to that of children in a nearby wealthier county. What was intended as a fair policy is working in an unfair way, causing unequal opportunity.

Who is responsible for social sin? We frequently hear the complaint that people today should not be blamed for the sins of the past, such as slavery. Yes, it would be unfair to blame anyone for the sins of the past. However, if we have inherited an unfair situation, then all members of society share responsibility for creating a more just society, and those people with the most opportunity bear the greatest responsibility. They are not to blame for the past, but they are responsible for doing what they can do now to make the present situation more fair.

As Christians, we are called to live the Lord's Prayer: "Thy kingdom come, thy will be done on earth as it is in heaven." That is all one sentence. The second part explains the first. The kingdom is come whenever and wherever we live as citizens of that kingdom, with God as Lord of our lives. The kingdom only comes in as much as we do God's will on earth as it is done in heaven. (The prayer takes for granted that God's will is done in heaven.) The Lord's

Prayer is a particularly clear challenge to all of us who take our faith seriously! It is a prayer not just for God to do something but that we do something.

Discussion Questions:

• How has my awareness of my own sinfulness changed over the years? Have I grown? Have I become lax?

• Do I genuinely make Lent a penitential time? How? Do I fast or choose something else?

• Should our church community be more active in addressing any of the social sins of our society?

• Are there social sins within the church? If so, how can we address them?

Suggested Reading:

Paul E. Dinter, *Beyond Naïve Belief: The Bible and Adult Catholic Faith* (New York: Crossroad, 1994), especially p. 238-251, on natural law. This book is difficult reading and not for everyone, but the author does an excellent job of bringing critical reason and modern knowledge into dialogue with our Christian faith tradition. He manages to maintain the believer's stance of loyalty to core Christian faith, which is timeless, while at the same time quite pointedly being critical of interpretations of that faith that seem crippled by the outdated scientific, or pre-scientific, beliefs of earlier times.

CHAPTER TWELVE

Heaven and Related Beliefs

Contents
This chapter will look briefly at the beliefs in heaven, hell, purgatory, and the kingdom of God.

There are some questions which are universal, asked by people in every culture, religion, and age in history. What happens to us? Is there life after death? Is there any connection between the way I live now and what happens to me after death?

There has been a very widespread belief, seen in different forms in different religions, that there is something about us that is immortal, that continues to exist even after the body dies. It is also common to find some belief that the way one acts in this life does in some way decide our fate in the next.

At the time of Jesus, some Jews believed in an individual resurrection of the dead, but that was not a universal Jewish belief. Some believed in a communal salvation; the people of God would be saved, and live on in their sons and daughters, in an earthly kingdom under God's protection. Many people in the ancient world believed that spirits of all the dead, good and bad, existed in a shadowy nether world, or sheol, beneath the earth. In Christian tradition, this gradually developed into our familiar concepts of heaven for the good and hell for the bad. Eventually, medieval theologians added the concept of purgatory to account for those of us who are not so wicked that we should be condemned to eternal punishment in hell, nor yet perfected and ready to be joined with God in heaven. Purgatory (the root word is "purge" or cleanse) was a place for most of us to be purified after death, knowing we are still somewhat sinful but expecting to be saved by God's goodness. In the Middle Ages, a fourth concept arose, limbo, a place for babies who died unbaptized. It was a place or state of no suffering for those who did not qualify for heaven but did not deserve any punishment. The belief in limbo was never a formal teaching of the church, but it seemed to be logical because of the literal belief that baptism was necessary for entrance into heaven. We are much more aware today that God is not limited to our celebration of the sacraments; God can save people who have not been baptized. As a result, the whole concept of limbo has now been dropped.

Scripture has references to heaven and hell, though it does not say much about them. It also has many references to "the kingdom of God," which is sometimes equated with heaven. We will look more closely at our beliefs about heaven, hell, purgatory, and the kingdom of God.

The first thing we might observe is that heaven and hell are heavily symbol-laden concepts. Most of it is very natural symbolism, found in many cultures. The fourteenth century Italian poet Dante also contributed a lot to our popular images in his well-known work, *The Divine Comedy*, which tours hell, purgatory, and heaven.

Heaven is up in the sky, light, in the warm sun where birds fly: all pleasant symbols of life and freedom. Halos of light are painted around saints. Angels have wings. In most religions the gods are up, either in the sky or on high mountains, where they can see everything. People have always envied the freedom of birds, which can fly away from danger up into that pleasant realm of the sky.

Hell, on the other hand, is under the earth where decaying things are, confining and miserable, dark, like a cold, slimy, pitch black cave in which one can be permanently trapped. The devil is often symbolized as a snake, condemned to crawling on the ground (Gn 3:14). Hell also picked up the image of fire, possibly from the constantly burning (and stinking) trash piles of ancient cities, into which unwanted bodies might also be thrown. Fire suggests pain, suffering, and misery.

We are very familiar with all this imagery. It is so ingrained in our culture that virtually everyone knows the images, even if they know nothing else about religion. (People remember images. That is why they are used.) But what are we really supposed to believe?

Most people brought up in a scientific culture today do not believe in heaven and hell as literal places, but the traditional symbols give a feeling for the meaning intended. We believe that the good find peaceful union with God, and that those who are totally self-centered and reject God exile themselves to an unhappy state of alienation and misery. We use the language of place and time because that is life as we know it, but after death there is no place or time. Time is a measurement of life cycles, decay rates, revolutions, and so on. It is a measurement of things happening in the material world and has no meaning in the spiritual world. Likewise spirits do not occupy space. We say God is everywhere; we could just as easily say that God is not anywhere; "where" is a designation of space, which is only relevant to material things. Movies may show ghosts as some sort of vaporous cloud, but that is because we want to see something when we watch a movie. However, Catholics and other mainline Christians do not generally believe there is any material substance to spirits or souls, therefore they are not "in" any particular place. Since the only world we know is the material world of time and space, we find it difficult to think or speak without reference to these concepts, so all of our imagery speaks of heaven and hell in terms of time and space.

St. Paul told the early Christians "Eye has not seen, and ear has not heard...what God has prepared for those who love him"(1 Cor 2:9). Paul was saying that we cannot describe what heaven—that peaceful, joyous union with God—will be like because it is unlike the life we know.

The Kingdom of God

One frequently recurring biblical image is the kingdom of God, often equated with heaven. There was a long-standing Jewish tradition that Jerusalem would one day be a reformed kingdom under God's reign, to which all peoples of the world would come in peace. Today some people, such as the Jehovah's Witnesses, believe the kingdom of God is a future redeemed earth, which good people will enjoy without death or suffering. But most Christians do not think of heaven as being on this earth. Science tells us that this life is inherently mortal. All physical life, even the earth itself, is part of an ever changing and temporary existence. Heaven, our hope in eternal peace in union with God and others, is beyond this existence we know.

If we read the gospels carefully, we find that there is much more to the kingdom. In the gospels, the kingdom of God is not a place. The kingdom is sometimes translated as the kingship of God or the reign of God. The Lord's Prayer is our best clue to the meaning of the kingdom. "Thy kingdom come, thy will be done on earth as it is in heaven." The kingdom will come whenever and wherever we do God's will on earth. In other words, the kingdom is not about a place or time somewhere else in the future, it is about our relationship with God. We are praying that we will recognize the reign of God and live as subjects of that kingship of God, doing God's will. This new relationship does not exist only after we die. When we allow God to be Lord of our lives, then we are living in the kingdom right here and now.

Discussion Questions:

• What is my image of heaven? How do I believe people get to heaven?

• What kingdom of God do I hope for? What does the Lord's Prayer mean to me?

• How do my beliefs about heaven, hell, or the kingdom of God shape my daily life?

CHAPTER THIRTEEN

Holiness in the Real World

Contents

This chapter will attempt to find a practical definition of holiness and discover how holiness can be attained in the ordinary "worldly" life.

Most Christians would agree that we are called to be holy. If we are called to be holy, what exactly does that mean? Most of us Catholics remember traditional holy pictures with Jesus, Mary, or the saints looking "other worldly," staring off into some unseen distance. We might have wondered if they weren't a bit out of touch with the real world of people, problems, and decisions that we face each day.

But Jesus of Nazareth was very much in touch with real people and their problems. In the gospels, he uses many parables that speak of real life, and his moral teachings call for down-to-earth common sense. For example, he points out that anyone would pull his ox out of a ditch even on the Sabbath (Luke 14:5). Both Jewish and Christian Scriptures challenge believers to an authentic way of everyday life seeking to live God's will. The earlier Jewish prophets reminded people that God is more interested in the way we treat the poor than in offerings at the temple. (See the book of Isaiah, 1:11–16.) So to begin, true holiness is a way of living, not a set of religious practices.

But what way of life is truly holy? Many of us grew up with the idea that those who truly sought holiness became priests or nuns. A generation ago, there was a sharp distinction in people's minds between the religious and lay worlds. We still hear the words religious life used to refer to the select few:

priests, nuns, and brothers in vowed orders. Priests, nuns, and brothers were considered to be separated from the busy everyday concerns of the rest of us. Also, these religious were dedicated to loving God, not dividing their loyalties between God and another person in marriage. (Saint Paul seems to have been of this mind. He recommended that people keep free of marriage and its burdens if they could handle that.) In comparison, we often considered lay people to be second class Christians, whose responsibilities to the world distracted us from God.

But what does the Bible say? If we remember the teachings of Jesus and Isaiah, what God cares most about is our practical care for our neighbor, not religious services. God is interested in our considerate care of spouses, children, elderly parents, neighbors, coworkers, students, patients, customers, whomever we deal with in our everyday lives. This is more important than how many church services we attend. We go to church services to be nourished by Christ who is our sustenance, to be reminded of who we are, so that we will be able to focus clearly on God's will for our everyday life.

Also, we might again note that marriage is recognized as a sacrament. In other words, the marriage relationship can be a profound sign of God's love, a sign for all Christians to see, lived out in ordinary family relationships. ("Can be"—we know not every marriage images God.) This is a recognition that ordinary life is meant to be holy.

Since Vatican II, the church has been trying to renew our awareness that all Christians are called by baptism to share in Christ's priesthood. All Christians are called to be other Christs, and there is no second class Christ! We are all called to holiness.

Another way to approach the topic is by looking at the meaning of the word "holy." It is helpful to note that the words "whole," "holy," and "heal" are derived from the same Old English roots. This logically suggests something common in their meaning. Jesus healed people to make them whole. He healed their bodies, but more importantly, that physical healing was a sign of the spiritual healing that also took place. He often cured people of blindness or deafness, which especially symbolize the failure to understand God's truth, the truth which points the way to our wholeness/happiness.

There is another word, taken from mathematics, that can help here, too. A whole number is called an integer. What words are related to integer? To integrate is to put things together in a whole. Integrity is being honest: meaning what you do, doing what you say; having mind and body, word and action, working together. Some years ago, there was a popular expression, a "together person" or "a person who had it all together" which really meant the same thing.

To put all of this together, holiness is wholeness, spiritual wholeness. It includes integrity, the wholeness of knowing who we are in relationship to God and others and living according to our beliefs. To be holy is to be healed of the brokenness and alienation of sin. To be holy is to be whole!

If we wish to be holy, it is important to pray because that helps us clarify our focus; it helps us find God at our center and helps us allow God to guide our decisions. This is how we seek wholeness, integrity. Christians who are holy pray, but they also live what they pray. They go to church to celebrate God as Lord of their lives, and they leave church to be guided by God in their daily decisions about family, job, neighbors, and possessions. Holy people realize that time, talents, and wealth are all gifts from God, and that we are stewards, not owners, of these gifts. We are challenged to use these gifts wisely for the good of all. If our prayer is genuine, it will help us recognize God as Lord of our everyday lives, relationships, work, and even leisure. This is true whether it is the priest or the bus driver deciding how to spend his time, talents, or money. Holiness is recognizing God as God and living accordingly. This is a simple, universal call. Not an easy call, since it challenges us to let God be God when our human tendency, as shown in the story of Adam and Eve, is to think we can run our lives without God. But the call to holiness is a universal call for all people. Christians have the greeting "God be with you!" (which, in the abbreviated style of the English became "Good-bye"). If we seek holiness, we should seek a constant sense of God with us, guiding us. This sense of God guiding us in all things is what Mother Teresa of Calcutta was getting at when she said she was called to faithfulness.

Discussion Questions:
- Which people do I think of as examples of holiness?
- How do I seek holiness?
- What factors in my life seem to make it difficult to be holy? What can I do to seek holiness in spite of those difficulties?

Final Note

This book is only a beginning. As the saying goes, "This is the first day of the rest of your life." Many of these topics are mysteries that we can ponder in awe and seek to better understand as long as we live. I hope I have successfully shared with you the sense that it does all fit together, and it is Good News. The gospel of Jesus is challenging, not easy. But it is not really a denial of self, as we often fear; it is a discovery of self. The more we surrender control to God, the more we discover how much God has empowered us. The more we give of ourselves, the more we discover that we have what we need and more. The first step is really believing that it is Good News.

Of Related Interest

Blessed Are You!
A Prayerbook for Catholics

Gwen Costello

This unique and deeply moving prayers offer Catholics a way to tap into their rich prayer tradition while also praying in contemporary terms. The morning and evening prayers can be prayed in as little as ten minutes and yet infuse the day with God's presence. There are also seasonal prayers, prayers to and from the saints, prayers for special needs and occasions, and the stations of the cross. Hardbound with ribbon.

136 pp, $19.95 (order X-91) 1-58595-260-5

The Joy and the Challenge
Reflections on the Readings for the 50 Days of Easter

Rev. Laurin J. Wenig

In his down-to-earth yet profound reflections Fr. Wenig brings the reader back to the first days of Christianity, when the disciples were struggling with the life, death, and resurrection of Jesus and all that it meant for their lives. He helps unfold that same mystery in life today and shows how to face the challenge and savor the joy of the paschal mystery. **The Joy and the Challenge** is an ideal companion for RCIA neophytes and leaders.

144 pp, $12.95 (order X-85) 1-58595-255-9

Questions & Answers for Catholics
Challenging; Contemporary, Vatican II
Msgr. James Songy

The questions here reflect the concerns of people who have asked about the core of the Catholic faith, the answers spring from the pastoral warmth and wisdom of the author.

1-58595-110-2, 288 pp, $14.95 (J-71)

Catholic Customs and Traditions
A Popular Guide
Greg Dues

From Candlemas, to the Easter candle, through relics, Mary, the saints, indulgences, the rosary, mystagogia, laying on of hands, and more, the author traces the vast riches of the traditions, customs, and rituals of Roman Catholics.

0-89622-515-1, 224 pp, $12.95 (C-14)

TWENTY-THIRD PUBLICATIONS

185 WILLOW STREET • PO BOX 180 • MYSTIC, CT 06355
TEL: 1-800-321-0411 • FAX: 1-800-572-0788
E-MAIL: ttpubs@aol.com • www.twentythirdpublications.com